THE HAMLYN LE

FIFTY-SECOND SERIES

DOES THE UNITED KINGDOM STILL HAVE A CONSTITUTION?

AUSTRALIA
LBC Information Services
Sydney

CANADA and USA
Carswell
Toronto, Ontario

NEW ZEALAND
Brooker's
Auckland

SINGAPORE and MALAYSIA
Sweet & Maxwell Asia
Singapore and Kuala Lumpur

DOES THE UNITED KINGDOM STILL HAVE A CONSTITUTION?

by

ANTHONY KING
Essex County Council Millennium
Professor of British Government,
University of Essex

Published under the auspices of
THE HAMLYN TRUST

LONDON
SWEET & MAXWELL
2001

Published in 2001 by Sweet & Maxwell Limited of
100 Avenue Road, Swiss Cottage,
London NW3 3PF
Typeset by LBJ Typesetting Ltd of Kingsclere
Printed in England by
MPG Books Ltd, Bodmin, Cornwall

No natural forests were destroyed to make this product;
only farmed timber was used and replanted

A CIP catalogue record for this book is available from the British Library

ISBN 0421 752009 (HB)
0421 74930X (PB)

To the members and officers of the Essex County Council

PREFACE

The four chapters of this book are based on the Hamlyn Lectures delivered at the Institute of Advanced Legal Studies in London in late November and early December 2000. It was a great honour, especially for a non-lawyer, to be invited to give the lectures, and I am enormously grateful to the Hamlyn Trustees both for extending the initial invitation and for taking great care with the organisation of the lectures. As may be imagined, it was more than a little daunting to be asked to join the company of Hamlyn Lecturers, a company including Lord Denning, Lord Scarman, Lord Justice Woolf and Lord Justice Sedley, among many other distinguished jurists. I only hope that the Hamlyn Trustees do not regret admitting into their midst a mere political scientist.

I also owe a debt of gratitude to the members and officers of the Essex County Council, to whom this book is dedicated, and especially to Lord Hanningfield, Ken Jones, Mervyn Juliff and Stewart Ashurst, the Chief Executive Officer. Led by Lord Hanningfield, it was they who had the imagination to recognise that the British constitution is undergoing a period of rapid and profound change, with cumulative consequences that are almost impossible to predict. They recommended to the County Council that, as one of Essex's contributions to the 2000 Millennium celebrations, the Council should endow a new Chair at the University of Essex specialising in constitutional change. Their recommendation was accepted. There can be few other local authorities anywhere in the world that have shown similar disinterestedness and vision. It is a great honour to be the first holder of the new Chair.

In preparing the lectures and this book, I profited immensely from the efficient and intelligent research assistance provided by two doctoral candidates at Essex University: first Jack Kneeshaw and then Rob Kemp. I am also grateful to Lord Neill of Bladen, Peter Riddell, Lord Justice Dyson (as he now is) and John Bridge, the chairman of the Hamlyn Trustees, for chairing the four lectures. Not least, I am grateful to six friends who read the manuscript in whole or in part and made valuable comments and suggestions: Sir John Dyson, Emma Gilmour, Jan King, Peter Riddell, Albert Weale and Sir Michael Wheeler-Booth. All six are granted the usual absolution. They did their best.

I should perhaps explain that this book is essentially a "think piece". It makes no claims to scholarly rigour and thoroughness; at many points it certainly eschews scholarly caution. Instead, it looks down on the United Kingdom's changing constitutional landscape from a high altitude, so to speak, seeking to identify the changing landscape's main features and ignoring much of the detail that inevitably looms larger closer to the ground. A fuller, more detailed and more nuanced study of the subject will be published by the Oxford University Press in 2002.

In the same spirit, I have resisted the (very great) temptation to festoon these pages with footnotes and references. I realised early on that, if I yielded to that temptation, almost every page of text would be cluttered with about two dozen reference numbers. It has seemed better to allow the argument to speak for itself and to confine the references mainly to direct quotations and matters of statistics. Fortunately, most of the facts set out in these pages are reasonably well known. It is the patterns that they make that the book as a whole seeks to draw attention to.

I should perhaps also confess that at two or three points I have allowed familiar political lore to take precedence over strict historical accuracy. For instance, in Chapter 3 I quote an unnamed politician as saying, "The man in Whitehall knows best." What Douglas Jay actually said in 1947 was: "For in the case of nutrition and health, just as in the case of education, the gentleman in Whitehall really does know better what is good for people than the people know themselves." I defend myself on the grounds that the familiar version is pithier than the strictly accurate version and better captures the spirit of the *Zeitgeist*.

Any reader wishing to take issue with any of my factual statements or interpretative judgments should feel free to write to me at the Department of Government, University of Essex, Wivenhoe Park, Colchester CO4 3SQ.

A.K.
December 18, 2000

TABLE OF CONTENTS

THE HAMLYN LECTURES

1949 Freedom under the Law
by the Rt Hon. Lord Denning

1950 The Inheritance of the Common Law
by Richard O'Sullivan, Esq.

1951 The Rational Strength of English Law
by Professor F.H. Lawson

1952 English Law and the Moral Law
by Professor A.L. Goodhart

1953 The Queen's Peace
by Sir Carleton Kemp Allen

1954 Executive Discretion and Judicial Control
by Professor C.J. Hamson

1955 The Proof of Guilt
by Professor Glanville Williams

1956 Trial by Jury
by the Rt Hon. Lord Devlin

1957 Protection from Power under English Law
by the Rt Hon. Lord MacDermott

1958 The Sanctity of Contracts in English Law
by Professor Sir David Hughes Parry

1959 Judge and Jurist in the Reign of Victoria
by C.H.S. Fifoot, Esq.

1960 The Common Law in India
by M.C. Setalvad, Esq.

1961 British Justice: The Scottish Contribution
by Professor Sir Thomas Smith

1962 Lawyer and Litigant in England
by the Rt Hon. Sir Robert Megarry

1963 Crime and the Criminal Law
by the Baroness Wootton of Abinger

1964 Law and Lawyers in the United States
by Dean Erwin N. Griswold

1965 New Law for a New World?
by the Rt Hon. Lord Tanley

1966 Other People's Law
by the Rt Hon. Lord Kilbrandon

1967 The Contribution of English Law to South African Law: and the Rule of Law in South Africa
by the Hon. O.D. Schreiner

1968 Justice in the Welfare State
by Professor H. Street

1969 The British Tradition in Canadian Law
by the Hon. Bora Laskin

1970 The English Judge
by Henry Cecil

1971 Punishment, Prison and the Public
by Professor Sir Rupert Cross

1972 Labour and the Law
by Professor Sir Otto Kahn-Freund

1973 Maladministration and its Remedies
by Sir Kenneth Wheare

1974 English Law—the New Dimension
by the Rt Hon. Lord Scarman

1975 The Land and the Development; or, The Turmoil and the Torment
by Sir Desmond Heap

1976 The National Insurance Commissioners
by Sir Robert Micklethwait

1977 The European Communities and the Rule of Law
by Lord Mackenzie Stuart

1978 Liberty, Law and Justice
by Professor Sir Norman Anderson

1979 Social History and Law Reform
by Professor Lord McGregor of Durris

1980 Constitutional Fundamentals
by Professor Sir William Wade

1981 Intolerable Inquisition? Reflections on the Law of Tax
by Hubert Monroe

1982 The Quest for Security: Employees, Tenants, Wives
by Professor Tony Honoré

1983 Hamlyn Revisited: The British Legal System Today
by Lord Hailsham of St Marylebone

1984 The Development of Consumer Law and Policy—Bold Spirits and Timorous Souls
by Sir Gordon Borrie

1985 Law and Order
by Professor Ralf Dahrendorf

1986 The Fabric of English Civil Justice
by Sir Jack Jacob

1987 Pragmatism and Theory in English Law
by P.S. Atiyah

1988 Justification and Excuse in the Criminal Law
by J.C. Smith

1989 Protection of the Public—A New Challenge
by the Rt Hon. Lord Justice Woolf

1990 The United Kingdom and Human Rights
by Dr Claire Palley

1991 Introducing a European Legal Order
by Gordon Slynn

1992 Speech & Respect
by Professor Richard Abel

1993 The Administration of Justice
by Lord Mackay of Clashfern

1994 Blackstone's Tower: The English Law School
by Professor William Twining

1995 From the Test Tube to the Coffin: Choice and Regulation in Private Life
by the Hon. Mrs Justice Hale

1996 Turning Points of the Common law
by the Rt Hon. The Lord Cooke of Thorndon KBE

1997 Commercial Law in the Next Millennium
by Professor Roy Goode

1998 Freedom Law and Justice
by the Rt Hon. Lord Justice Sedley

1999 The State of Justice
by Michael Zander Q.C.

THE HAMLYN TRUST

The Hamlyn Trust owes its existence to the will of the late Miss Emma Warburton Hamlyn of Torquay, who died in 1941 at the age of 80. She came of an old and well-known Devon family. Her father, William Bussell Hamlyn, practised in Torquay as a solicitor and J.P. for many years, and it seems likely that Miss Hamlyn founded the trust in his memory. Emma Hamlyn was a woman of strong character, intelligent and cultured, well-versed in literature, music and art, and a lover of her country. She travelled extensively in Europe and Egypt, and apparently took considerable interest in the law and ethnology of the countries and cultures that she visited. An account of Miss Hamlyn by Dr Chantal Stebbings of the University of Exeter may be found, under the title "The Hamlyn Legacy", in volume 42 of the published lectures.

Miss Hamlyn bequeathed the residue of her estate on trust in terms which it seems were her own. The wording was thought to be vague, and the will was taken to the Chancery Division of the High Court, which in November 1948 approved a Scheme for the administration of the trust. Paragraph 3 of the Scheme, which closely follows Miss Hamlyn's own wording, is as follows:

> "The object of the charity is the furtherance by lectures or otherwise among the Common People of the United Kingdom of Great Britain and Northern Ireland of the knowledge of the Comparative Jurisprudence and Ethnology of the Chief European countries including the United Kingdom, and the circumstances of the growth of such jurisprudence to the Intent that the Common People of the United Kingdom may realise the privileges which in law and custom they enjoy in comparison with other European Peoples and realising and appreciating such privileges may recognise the responsibilities and obligations attaching to them."

The Trustees are to include the Vice-Chancellor of the University of Exeter, representatives of the Universities of London, Leeds, Glasgow, Belfast and Wales and persons co-opted. At present there are nine Trustees:

From the outset it was decided that the objects of the Trust could best be achieved by means of an annual course of public lectures of outstanding interest and quality by eminent Lecturers, and by their subsequent publication and distribution to a wider audience. The first of these Lectures were delivered by the Rt Hon. Lord Justice Denning (as he then was) in 1949. Since then there has been an unbroken series of annual Lectures. A complete list of the Lectures may be found on pages vii to x. The Trustees have also, from time to time, provided financial support for a variety of projects which, in various ways, have disseminated knowledge or have promoted a wider public understanding of the law. One such project, undertaken by the Centre for Criminal Justice Studies of the University of Leeds, has produced the website "U.K. Law Online: The U.K. Legal System on the Internet": see http://www.leeds.ac.uk/law/hamlyn/.

This, the 52nd series of Lectures, was delivered by Professor Anthony King at the Institute of Advanced Legal Studies of the University of London in November and December 2000.

January 2001 **JOHN BRIDGE**
Chairman of the Trustees

1. TWO CONSTITUTIONAL ARCHETYPES

A book on the future of the British constitution, even a short book like this one, needs to begin by offering a definition of the word "constitution". Here is the definition that will be used throughout the remainder of this chapter and the ones that follow:

> A constitution is the set of the most important rules that regulate the relations among the different parts of the government of a given country and also the relations between the different parts of the government and the people of the country.

That definition is far from perfect—for example, it says nothing about a country's international commitments—but it will do for our purposes.

Although our proposed definition may strike some readers as mundane, perhaps even humdrum, it has a number of important implications, one or two of which are fairly obvious but one or two of which most definitely are not.

One of the obvious implications is that, in any discussion of a country's constitution, a good deal will turn on the meaning of the phrase "the *most important* rules". Some rules undeniably fall into that category: in the United Kingdom, for instance, the rule that says that free and fair elections must be held from time to time. Equally undeniably, some rules, although they *are* rules, do not fall into that category: for instance, the rule requiring the Speaker of the House of Commons to wear a black gown and the Lord Chancellor when presiding over the Upper House to wear a black silk gown and a full-bottomed wig. But inevitably there will be difficult and more marginal cases that are open to dispute. Between 1918 and 1928, for instance, the democratic franchise was at long last extended to women in the United Kingdom on the same terms as men. The change was undoubtedly desirable; it was undoubtedly important to large numbers of women. It marked a fundamental change in the way in which women were viewed, and viewed themselves, in British society.

But was it a *constitutional* change? Probably not. The character of the relations between governors and governed in the UK remained substantially unaltered.

A simple analogy with football may help to clarify the point. The off-side rule in football is clearly one of the most important rules in the game—part of its "constitution", so to speak. To abandon or drastically amend the off-side rule would be fundamentally to change the game's character (for the worse, needless to say). But the rule governing the tossing of a coin to decide which side will kick off a match is equally clearly not one of the game's most important rules. To change that rule (within reason) would be to change very little. In between, and more arguably, come the rules governing the precise width of the goal mouth in football and whether or not penalties should be awarded for professional fouls. Fortunately, this book deals only with what are incontestably the United Kingdom's most important constitutional rules.

One reason for laying so much stress on the question of importance in discussing constitutional issues is that much of the ink spilt in this country on allegedly constitutional matters—by constitutional experts, constitutional lawyers and others—is concerned with what are in reality rather peripheral matters. To take the most obvious example, the Monarchy and the monarch have long since ceased to feature significantly in British political life—as distinct from British symbolism and British history—yet a substantial proportion of the scholarly writings on the United Kingdom's constitution is still devoted to discussions of the monarch's role in that constitution. To be sure, there are circumstances in which the actions and decisions of the monarch might, for a time, become important; but these circumstances are exceedingly rare. The fact is that many of the subjects discussed by constitutional experts, often in an arcane way, are *not* of central constitutional importance.

The use of the specific word "rules" in our proposed definition is also worth pausing over. A constitution is a set of rules (which, like all rules, may or may not be broken from time to time); however, a constitution is not, and does not purport to be, a full and accurate description of the power relations currently prevailing in any given society. To revert to the football analogy, the rules of football govern the way the game is played, but they have nothing to say about which are the better sides in the English or Scottish premierships, nor do they have anything to say about who will win Saturday's match between Ipswich Town and Newcastle United. The rules, in that sense, are neutral. For example, any full account of the power relations in

British society in the 1970s would have had to include an account of the political role of the trade unions. But in the 1980s Margaret Thatcher marginalised the unions, and the power balance in the UK accordingly shifted. But it would be odd—and clearly inappropriate—to say that the United Kingdom's *constitution* had changed.

But the final point to be made about our seemingly humdrum definition is the least obvious and at the same time, by a wide margin, the most important.

It is this. Constitutions, as we are defining them, are never—to repeat, *never*—written down. They might possibly in principle be written down, but in practice they never are. There are, of course, written documents called Constitutions—with a capital 'C'—but they are never, ever coextensive with all of a country's most important rules regulating the relations between different parts of the government and those between the government and the people. Constitutions as defined here and the written documents called Constitutions overlap to a greater or lesser degree. Of course they do: all capital-C Constitutions have at least *some* bearing on how the countries that have them are actually governed. But capital-C Constitutions and small-c constitutions are never the same thing, and sometimes the relationship between the two is quite tenuous (even if, in a given country, the capital-C Constitution is taken seriously).

The relationship between a constitution and a Constitution is illustrated in a shorthand manner by the diagram (See diagram on next page). The specific relationship depicted in the diagram points to a considerable degree of overlap between constitution and Constitution; but, depending on the country and the historical era in question, the overlap could be substantially greater or substantially less. One important instance of a real-world overlap—many others could be cited—concerns the article of America's capital-C Constitution that provides that "the President shall be Commander in Chief of the Army and Navy of the United States". That article of America's capital-C Constitution is clearly also an important feature of America's small-c constitution. It enabled President Truman in 1951, for example, to sack General Douglas MacArthur as commander of US forces in Korea; it enabled Presidents Johnson and Nixon to fight the Vietnam War in the way that they did. There is no suggestion here that capital-C constitutions are necessarily and always irrelevant. Such a suggestion would be absurd. All that is being asserted here is that the degree of overlap between the two kinds of constitution is a matter of contingent fact, to be ascertained on a case-by-case basis. And the overlap—to make the same point yet again—is *never* total.

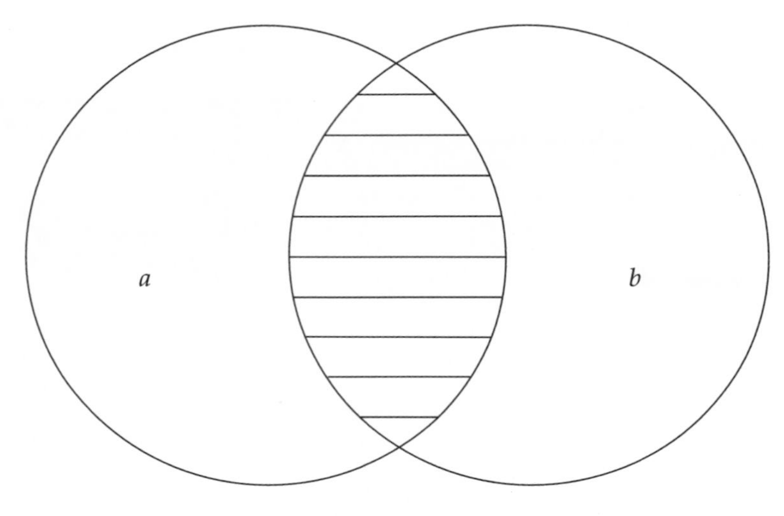

This lack of overlap between constitutions and Constitutions—between the important rules and the ones that happen to have been written down in a codified document—takes two forms: what written Constitutions leave out that true constitutions take in (zone *a* in the diagram) and what written Constitutions take in that true constitutions leave out (zone *b* in the diagram). Both the omissions of written Constitutions (zone *a*) and their often otiose inclusions (zone *b*) are easily illustrated.

Take the omissions first. They are far more important. In every democratic country, by universal consent, the electoral system—the way in which the people's votes are cast, counted and (usually) translated into parliamentary seats—is one of the most important of the prevailing political rules. The kind of electoral system a country has profoundly influences both the pattern of political competition in that country and the way in which the governments of that country come into being and subsequently wield power. One has only to compare the United Kingdom with, say, Israel or Italy to see that that is so. Yet there is almost no country with a Constitution that includes the electoral system among its formal constitutional provisions. No small-c constitution is, or could possibly be, silent on the subject:

every democratic country has, and must have, some kind of electoral system. But capital-C Constitutions are typically silent on the subject—completely silent. For all their formal elegance, capital-C Constitutions are often strangely circumscribed in terms of their contents. Most such Constitutions also have little or nothing to say about political parties, even though they are essential to the workings of small-c constitutions.

This general point is splendidly illustrated by the American capital-C Constitution, the world's best known. Not only is the US Constitution silent on most aspects of the American electoral system (and actually misleading on several of the others), not only does it make no mention of political parties, but it also makes no reference to another of the most important features of America's small-c constitution: namely, the undoubted power of the US Supreme Court to declare Acts of the American Congress unconstitutional: that is, in violation of the capital-C Constitution. This power of the US Supreme Court is clearly an absolutely crucial power. It has been used, among many other things, to outlaw racial segregation in American schools and to legalise abortion. But the Supreme Court was not given this power under the Constitution. Led by Chief Justice John Marshall, in the case of *Marbury v. Madison* in 1803, the Court's justices simply took it: they simply arrogated the power to themselves. In other words, without in any way amending America's capital-C Constitution, they drastically amended its small-c constitution, in the sense of creating one of America's "most important rules".

The corresponding point—that capital-C Constitutions frequently include elements that are *not* among a country's most important rules—is also easily illustrated. For instance, the Austrian constitution solemnly declares that:

> The federal Coat of Arms consists of an unfettered single-headed, black, gilt-armed and red-tongued eagle on whose breast is imposed a red shield intersected by a silver crosspiece. On its head, the eagle bears a mural crown with three visible merlons. A sundered iron chain rings both talons. The right holds a golden sickle with inward turned blade, the left a golden hammer.

To take a quite different example, the Greek constitution solemnly states that "the alteration of the contents or conditions of a will, codicil or donations, so far as its provisions in favour of the State or the public benefit are concerned, shall be prohibited." But no one imagines for a moment that whether or not the Austrian eagle's three merlons are visible or whether or not Greek wills involving the state can be altered are really matters of constitutional significance, at least on our definition of the word. Nor, on this definition, is it a matter of genuine constitutional significance that in Iceland "the President of the Republic shall reside in or near Reykjavik." To repeat: capital-C Constitutions are almost as remarkable for the odd things they include as for what they leave out.

What, then, is the upshot of all this for a discussion of the future of our own constitution? That is an easy question to answer. The answer falls into two parts. The first is that anyone dealing with this subject should focus on, and only on, the most important of our political rules, whatever precise form—written or unwritten, statutory or conventional—those rules take. The second is that the fact that the United Kingdom does not yet possess a capital-C Constitution of the American, French or German type is neither here nor there. Many of our most important rules—for example, those governing the legal life of Parliaments and the powers of the House of Lords—*are* written down. Many others—for example, the one that secures the prime ministership for the leader of the largest party in the House of Commons—are not. The differences between the two are entirely ones of form. They are scarcely at all ones of substance.

The important point is not whether we do or do not have a capital-C Constitution (we clearly do not) or whether our most important rules are or are not written down (some of them are, some are not) but that we do, of course, have a constitution in the small-c sense. Or, rather, we used to have one. The purpose of this short book is to enquire whether we still have one and, if so, what kind of constitution it now is.

II

We begin our enquiry, however, not in the United Kingdom but in the abstract. To be able intelligently to assess constitutional change in this country, we need to have an appreciation of the constitutional possibilities that exist in other modern democracies—to have an appreciation of the various constitutional "options", so to speak, that are currently available. We also need to have an understanding of how democracy actually works in at least one country whose constitution—in the small-c sense—differs significantly from our own. Kipling famously wrote in *The English Flag*: "And what should they know of England who only England know?" He was righter than he knew. It is impossible to understand the politics of any country without some knowledge—indeed quite a detailed knowledge—of the politics of at least a few others.

A convenient way of launching our enterprise of constitutional comparison is to establish and consider two liberal democratic "archetypes": two ways of organising, and two styles of operating, the politics and government of a democracy. Neither of the two archetypes exists in a pure form anywhere in the real world; all real-world systems contain some elements of both, and all real-world systems also contain idiosyncratic, country-specific elements that are peculiar to themselves (the world being, as we know, a delightfully messy place). The purpose of archetypes—or "ideal-types", as the great German sociologist Max Weber called them—is not to *describe* anything or anywhere. It is, rather, to enable us to draw out the most significant features of real-world systems, partly by observing how well they do, and do not, accord with our archetypes.

Our first archetype is that of the "power-sharing" constitution. The power-sharing constitution, and the political norms and customs usually associated with it, have a number of salient characteristics. The single most important is that in such a constitutional regime there exist, within the governmental system itself, autonomous centres of political power. The institutions of government are to a considerable extent pluralist and fragmented. There is no single Hobbesian "sovereign".

This institutional fragmentation can take a geographical form, as it does, for example, in Switzerland, with substantial power residing in the Swiss confederation's 23 cantons, or the Federal Republic of Germany, with substantial power given over to the sixteen federal *Länder*; or it can take the form, as it does in the US, of deliberately contrived "checks and balances" among the different branches of government; or it can arise out of the fact that, in multi-party systems where coalition governments predominate, the various parties making up the coalition often become autonomous and powerful political actors in their own right. Most countries whose constitutions approximate to the power-sharing model—not all, but most—have proportional electoral systems, pluralist party systems and, more often than not, coalition governments.

But, whatever characteristics of a country give rise to this diffusion and fragmentation of power, the central point is that power-*holders* in such a system have no alternative but to be, in addition, power-*sharers*. Almost without exception, the actions and decisions of government are the result of bargaining, negotiating and all manner of pulling, hauling and deal-making, some of it dignified, some of it less so. In a power-sharing system, there are seldom outright winners and outright losers. The great majority of the participants get used to the idea of being partial winners and partial losers most of the time.

An additional feature of a power-sharing political system is that power sharing in practice usually comes to be associated with power sharing in principle. The political class in such a society is not only forced by circumstances to try to achieve a broad consensus: most of its members come in time to believe that achieving a broad consensus is desirable for its own sake. Agreement, including agreement among the political parties, is good, even when not strictly necessary; disagreement, while of course inevitable, is bad and should be minimised wherever possible. No intrinsic delight is taken in confrontation and contestation.

A number of manifestations of this kind of consensus-seeking political culture are worth noting. One is that in power-sharing democracies the inter-party coalition governments that are formed are frequently what political scientists call over-sized or surplus-majority coalitions—that is, coalitions that comprise more parties than are strictly necessary for the government to be sure of having a clear majority in the country's parliament. Even in circumstances where, for example, two parties would be in a position on their own to command an overall majority, the actual coalition governments that are formed frequently consist of three or four parties. To take an admittedly extreme case, in 1957 the Christian Democrats and the Bavarian Christian Social Union under Konrad Adenauer won an overall majority in the German Bundestag. They nevertheless chose to remain in coalition with the small *Deutsche Partei.*

Another manifestation of consensus seeking in power-sharing systems—supererogatory consensus seeking, so to speak, beyond what is strictly required by the current balance of political forces—is frequently found in the disposition to accord the opposition party or parties a role in policy making, even when, in parliamentary terms, their voices and votes are not essential. The parliaments in power-sharing systems, for instance, frequently have active and powerful committee systems, with the opposition parties represented on the committees and able to play a significant role in their work. In Japan, single-party rather than coalition governments have been the norm since 1947. Even so, the opposition parties are consulted about legislation, both before its introduction and during its passage through parliament, and the norms of Japanese politics require that even controversial bills be made as palatable to the opposition as possible. The Japanese sometimes go so far as to talk of an "opposition veto".

This desire to accommodate, this desire to embrace, often extends further, to the major interest aggregations in power-sharing democracies: business, labour, the farmers, the doctors, the lawyers, the teachers, the various religious denominations and so on. The representatives of these interests typically have a major role, often a formal role, in the making of government policy and sometimes also in its implementation. The borders between "government" and "non-government" often, in practice, become extremely blurred. The word "corporatism" is sometimes used to describe such arrangements. That is probably too strong, ascribing to the organised interest groups more power and greater cohesion than they commonly possess. But certainly the organised interests are typically more influential in power-sharing democracies than elsewhere—and their influence is typically regarded as being more legitimate, more "proper".

So much for our first archetype, the archetype of a power-sharing constitutional system, with pluralism, multiple centres of political power, constant efforts to accommodate different interests and opinions and a sustained desire to promote agreement and consensus.

What of our other archetype? If our first was of a power-sharing regime, our second might be said to be of a regime that is "power-hoarding". In a power-hoarding regime—the term needs no explanation—there are few or no autonomous centres of political power, apart from, in a liberal democracy, the voters themselves and possibly also the mass media. Political power in a power-hoarding political system is concentrated in the hands of the government, and the government is usually a single-party government. The courts have little autonomous power, and they certainly lack the power to declare unconstitutional acts that the government approves of. The national parliament also counts for little, and parliamentary committees in power-hoarding systems have little clout, being dominated for the most part by the government's own supporters. As for government officials—the civil service—they are there merely, in the end, to do the government's bidding. In a pure power-hoarding system, regional and local political structures are also invariably non-existent or weak (though it may be that, under a federal constitution, a regime that is largely power-hoarding at the national level, such as that of Australia, may have to share a modicum of power, perhaps quite a lot, with states or provinces).

Power-hoarding regimes are thus characterised by a concentration—and usually a centralisation—of political power. Not only that, but, just as in the case of our first archetype power-sharing institutions were associated with a power-sharing political culture, so, in the case of our second archetype, the institutions of a power-hoarding regime are associated closely with a political culture that legitimises and reinforces the hoarding of power. The guiding normative principle of our second archetype is "winner takes all". The main political parties may alternate in power, but, when Party A or Party B takes power in such a system, it takes it all—and it is thought entirely appropriate that this should be so. "To the victor", as the Americans used to say, "belong the spoils."

In particular, consensus seeking in such a culture is at a discount. The aim is not to compromise; it is to win. And winning means mobilising one's own troops against those of the enemy. The political style of a power-hoarding democracy is typically adversarial, even belligerent. Party A can do no right, Party B can do no wrong—or vice versa, according to taste. Debate is preferred to discussion, confrontation to negotiation. The opposition—often spelt with a capital "O"—is just that: the opposition. The opposition party or parties form no part of the governmental process. They are there to criticise and to condemn, not to make a constructive contribution. The representatives of organised interests are similarly kept at arm's length. They may lobby the government, and the government may listen to what the more important of them have to say; but, unlike the organised interests in a power-sharing system, they are not—or are only very seldom—integrated directly into the governmental apparatus.

The probable strengths and weaknesses of these two types of system can easily be guessed at, though whether they actually exhibit these strengths and weaknesses cannot be proved one way or the other since, for the moment, we are dealing only with archetypes and not with real-world examples.

A pure power-sharing democracy could be expected to display a certain deliberation in its policy-making processes. Policy discussions would be prolonged, with every conceivable body of opinion and organised interest group actively participating and with almost every conceivable option carefully considered. By the time a decision was finally reached, the fingerprints of almost everyone in the system would be upon it and it would be highly unlikely that any feasible policy option would have been overlooked.

Two benign consequences might be expected to follow. In the first place, the policy that eventually emerged—based on the most extensive consultation and compromise—might be expected to be country-uniting rather than country-dividing; the chances are that it would be broadly accepted as the best outcome available under all the circumstances. In the second place, precisely because the policy was generally, if not necessarily enthusiastically, accepted, it might be expected to stick, to remain the policy of the country for a considerable period of time. A power-sharing democracy would seem likely to exhibit considerable continuity in policy, with radical changes in, say, taxation policy or education policy occurring only rarely. As a wise observer of Swiss politics has remarked, "Most general [European] developments follow in the Helvetic Confederation after a discreet time-lag and no doubt when the end of the world comes it will be two days late in Altdorf and Schwyz."[1]

The outcomes in a power-sharing democracy might, however, be less benign. The dangers of delay would always be inherent in decision-making processes that either necessitated or valued (or both) careful consideration of every option and painstaking negotiations with every interested party. Haggling is almost invariably a time-consuming process. Moreover, even if a given policy were produced relatively quickly, it might, because it had been so extensively negotiated, turn out to be a bad policy; at worst, it might represent nothing more than a fudge, with difficult but essential policy choices failing to be confronted. Putting the same point another way, compromises can lead to optimal outcomes but they can also lead to sheer muddle. There is also the ever-present danger in a power-sharing system that, because there are so many powerholders, any one of them—as often happens in Israel—may succeed in wielding disproportionate influence. Their opportunities for blackmail may be legion; so may their opportunities for obstruction and delay. Successful power sharing depends on a willingness to work together and to compromise. Absent that willingness, much may go awry.

The potential strengths and weaknesses of the power-hoarding system are, not surprisingly, the obverse of those of the power-sharing system. Policy-hoarding regimes make it possible, though they by no means guarantee, that the content of government policy will be coherent and intelligible. They also greatly facilitate, though they by no means guarantee, speed of decision and decisiveness of action. Coalition-based regimes may be lumbering in their movements; power-hoarding regimes, especially governments based on only a single political party, may respond much more quickly to altered circumstances, including national crises. If a government in a power-hoarding system has a will, it will be uniquely well placed to impose it.

Every silver lining has a cloud, however, and speed and clarity of decision may not always yield the best results.

decisions under a power-hoarding regime may be erely speedily but hastily, perhaps under intense ure for the government "to do something". The hat, as a result, they do may be ill-considered and e been taken with due regard for administrative realities and any need that there may be for public consent. They may also be opposed by the Opposition, and, if they are, the Opposition may pledge itself to abandon or reverse the offending policy when it comes to power. Frequent and sometimes abrupt changes of policy might be expected to be a feature of power-hoarding regimes, as governments change their political complexion or incumbent governments recognise the errors of their over-hasty ways.

In addition, the decisions taken and the policies adopted, precisely because so few interests and parties have been actively engaged in their preparation, and because there are, therefore, so few fingerprints on them, may provoke opposition from the public and even riots and other acts of non-compliance. Power-hoarding regimes may turn out to be divisive regimes, magnifying differences within society rather than attempting to reconcile them.

Before we move on, one final point needs to be made in connection with our two archetypes: namely, that no significance whatsoever should be attached to the precise way in which they have been labelled. The word "sharing" in "power sharing" sounds comfortable, even cuddly. The word "hoarding" in "power hoarding" sounds mean, miserly and altogether unpleasant. But no commendation is meant in the former case, no offence in the latter. The two words were chosen partly because they do convey something of the true nature of the two regime-types and partly also because they convey more in this connection than any of the other words that might have been chosen.

III

But enough of archetypes. Back to the real world (though as we have gone along readers will undoubtedly have been supplying all manner of real-world referents for themselves). Although no modern democracy conforms exactly to either of our two archetypes, and although a few systems have to be regarded as hybrids, most systems do conform quite closely to either one archetype or the other. The archetypes turn out to have considerable descriptive value.

There is a real danger, however, that some readers—especially in the United Kingdom—may be inclined not to take the power-sharing archetype altogether seriously. They may find it hard to credit that such a system could exist and also function effectively. But there are, in fact, a number of liberal democratic regimes, out there in the real world, that do exhibit many of the features of the power-sharing archetype, and it is worth exploring in some detail how one of them works, if only to put some flesh on the bare bones of the analysis—the rather abstract analysis—that has been offered above.

The example chosen of a power-sharing regime is that of the Netherlands. The Netherlands is one of our nearest neighbours. The Dutch people look rather like us. We and the Dutch visit each other's countries frequently. Those in the Netherlands who speak English at all speak it rather better than we do. Not least, the Netherlands is, by every known measure, one of the world's most stable and successful democracies. The way in which the Dutch people conduct their politics therefore merits our attention.[2]

To an outsider, the Netherlands seems a remarkably placid country. The Dutch have a clear and unambiguous sense of national identity. They are Dutch, they know they are Dutch, and they are happy to be so; few have any desire to be anything else. The Netherlands suffers from none of the nationality problems—Basques in Spain, Corsicans in France, Flemish vs Walloons in Belgium—that beset other European countries. In addition, the Netherlands' economy is one of the world's most open, and the Dutch have known for generations that their country's prosperity depends on their ability to buy and sell in foreign markets. The existence of a broadly capitalist economic order is taken for granted. The Communist Party in the Netherlands has always been weak, far weaker than in, say, France or Italy.

At the same time, however, the Netherlands historically has been a divided country: united in wanting to continue to exist but divided along sectarian as well as class lines. To the class divisions common throughout Europe during the past century and a half have been added, in the Netherlands, divisions between Catholics and Protestants and between the two main Protestant denominations. The Netherlands' multi-party political system has always reflected these multiple divisions in Dutch society. Fortunately in some ways, it has always been clear that no single social or religious block was ever going to be in a position to command a national majority and that therefore every group in society was condemned to permanent minority status. The Netherlands' leaders accordingly evolved a structure and style of government that corresponds closely to our power-sharing archetype and is usually known to political scientists as "consociational democracy".[3]

The institutions of Dutch democracy bear an outward resemblance to those in almost all other democratic countries. Free and fair elections are held every three or four years. The elections are fought by national political parties. Following the elections, a new government is formed—or not, as the case may be. There is a prime minister and a cabinet. There is a two-chamber national parliament, in the Dutch case called the States-General (though with the more important of the two chambers called, confusingly, the Second Chamber). The parties in parliament usually vote along strict party lines. The head of state, as in most of Scandinavia and the Low Countries, is a constitutional monarch.

But, as soon as one begins to press one's enquiries, one discovers that all is not quite as it seems. One clue is provided by the connection—or, rather, the lack of connection—between the outcomes of elections in the Netherlands and the formation of governments. Dutch voters vote. Their votes are counted. Their votes are translated, on a highly proportional basis, into parliamentary seats. Then the process of government formation begins. And the significant point to note in this connection is that the process of government formation ultimately depends, not on the outcome of the preceding election in terms either of votes cast or of seats won, but on the way in which the leaders of the various political parties choose to view the current political situation overall and, in particular, their relations with the other parties. During the late 1970s and 1980s, for example, whenever the Dutch Labour Party gained seats in the Second Chamber at an election, it was expelled from the government that was subsequently formed and, whenever it lost seats, it was at once readmitted. The voice of the people may be the voice of God, but in the Netherlands God is obviously not in direct communion with the politicians.

Another clue is provided by the relations between the Dutch prime minister and the other members of the Dutch government, in particular the cabinet. Note the precise language used in the previous sentence: not "*his* government" or "*his* cabinet", but "*the* government" and "*the* cabinet", because the relations between Dutch prime ministers and Dutch governments and cabinets are much more egalitarian than the relations between prime ministers and governments in most other countries. There is a famous story, often told in Dutch political-science circles, of the distinguished Dutch political scientist who submitted an article to a British journal. He wrote in the article of Dutch ministers serving *with*, not *under*, the Dutch prime minister. Apparently it took him nearly an hour to persuade the journal's editor that he was not a foolish foreigner who could not speak English but that his choice of language was an accurate reflection of Dutch political realities.

What is this all about? The short answer is that it is about the Dutch tradition of, and the Dutch institutionalisation of, power sharing—specifically, power sharing among the members of the Dutch political elite. Everyone in the Netherlands knows that the winner will not take all, because there never is an outright winner. Everyone in the Netherlands also knows that, whichever parties are "in power" in the sense of forming the government, power will in reality be parcelled out, including to those outside the government. It will not be hoarded.

A variety of Dutch political institutions and ways of working illustrate the point. One has already been alluded to: the structure and workings of the Dutch cabinet, where the prime minister is not first among equals but little more than one of the equals. In many countries—the United Kingdom and France, for example—the cabinet has long since ceased to be a decision-making body and has become largely a decision-ratifying body. In those countries and others, the cabinet meets seldom, its meetings are quickly over, and little real business is transacted. In the Netherlands, by contrast, the cabinet is a relatively small body, it meets frequently, its meetings can last for hours, and the members of the cabinet, sitting around the table, take real decisions, often decisions that diverge from the initial proposals put before them. Moreover, again in conformity with the power-sharing archetype, Dutch cabinets since the war have frequently been "over-sized", not in the sense of being big but in the sense of containing representatives of more parties than are absolutely necessary to secure a parliamentary majority.

Seats around the cabinet table in the Netherlands are distributed on the basis of proportionality, with each governing party receiving seats in proportion to the size of its parliamentary contingent, and this "principle of proportionality" operates at almost every level of the Dutch system. Town mayors and provincial governors are not elected but, unusually, are appointed by the central government; but the central government, far from making appointments only from among members of the parties making up the coalition, frequently makes appointments from among the non-governing parties—in order to reflect, in a rough sort of way, all the political parties' national electoral strengths. Unsurprisingly, local government in the Netherlands is almost invariably coalition government, and the governing coalitions are frequently "mirror coalitions", with all the parties represented on the local council also represented—on a proportional basis, of course—in the local cabinet.

But perhaps the most extreme instance of the proportionality principle in action is the Dutch electoral system, already referred to. Although the Netherlands is quite a large country, with a population of nearly 16 million, the Dutch do not elect any of their members of parliament from geographically defined parliamentary constituencies, not even from large constituencies of the type common in PR systems. Instead, the whole country, from Groningen in the north to Maastricht in the south, constitutes one large constituency. The people's votes are cast locally but counted nationally, and each party is awarded seats in the Second Chamber strictly in proportion to its share of the national vote. There is no minimum threshold of votes which parties have to surmount before they can be represented in parliament, and small parties frequently win seats on the basis of minute fractions of the national vote (sometimes as little as one per cent).

This extreme form of PR in the Netherlands is not to be seen as solely the product of some historical accident. It has a moral underpinning. Two of the most perceptive and intelligent students of Dutch politics, Rudy Andeweg and Galen Irwin, observe that "proportionality has become so engrained in Dutch political culture that it has become almost synonymous with fairness." They add that "the Dutch are appalled when they learn how majority electoral systems in other countries, such as the UK and the USA, 'distort' election outcomes."[4]

The principles of proportionality and sharing out go hand in hand with another principle, unstated but almost universally practised in the Netherlands, that of inclusivity. Anyone or any group with an interest in the outcome of policy making is included in the policy-making process—or, more precisely, in one of the various policy-making processes, since the making of government policy is parcelled out in the Netherlands to a wide variety of functionally organised mini-governments, covering almost every aspect of the Dutch state's activities, from agriculture and labour law to education and health. These mini-governments invariably comprise representatives of the relevant government department or departments together with representatives of all the affected or likely-to-be-affected parties. As the power-sharing archetype suggested might happen, the line between "government" and "non-government" is blurred, sometimes to the point to being erased altogether. In the Netherlands, these mini-governments are much more than loose-textured policy networks: they usually take legal or quasi-legal institutional form, whether as advisory boards, tripartite councils or regulatory commissions. Andeweg and Irwin refer to there being a veritable "jungle" of such bodies.[5] The interests represented on them fight their corners, they differ, they argue; but the acknowledged aim is to reach agreements that all can accept; and every leading authority on Dutch politics and government agrees that their success rate is high. Once agreement has been reached, those involved in the discussions leading to the agreement accept collective responsibility for ensuring that it is put into effect.

This last point, concerning the implementation of policy, is important. In most countries, government decisions are just that, government decisions, and responsibility for implementing them lies with government departments and agencies. Not so in the Netherlands—or at least not uniformly so. In accordance with the principles of proportionality and sharing out, many of the functions that in other countries are performed by central government agencies—for example, in connection with the provision of health care—are performed in the Netherlands either by the inclusive advisory boards and tripartite councils referred to earlier or by church-related and other non-governmental organisations. In the case of the latter, funds are allocated, needless to say, on a proportional basis.

By now it will come as no surprise to the reader to learn that these institutional structures and practices are intertwined in the Netherlands with distinctive features of that nation's political culture. Neither institutions nor culture are conceivable without the other; they are part of the same package, so to speak.

To begin with, the word "compromise", which has almost wholly negative connotations in many countries, implying a willingness to dissimulate and to abandon one's principles, has no such connotations in the Netherlands. On the contrary, the Dutch regard a willingness to compromise and a reluctance to take up rigid, inflexible positions as a positive civic virtue, as being essential to the achievement of acceptable political outcomes. Politicians in many other countries never want to be found in compromising positions; Dutch politicians always do, so great is the Dutch desire to avoid discord and division and to be able to live comfortably together.

But, of course, differences of opinion and conflicts of interest are as endemic in the Netherlands as in most other democratic countries, and satisfactory compromises are not always easy, or even possible, to arrive at. The Dutch respond in a variety of ways, three of which are germane for our purposes.

One is that political leaders in the Netherlands should never, if at all possible, act in a hurry: no haste, no precipitancy, no snap decisions, certainly no ramming of controversial decisions down other people's throats. The Dutch not only make a virtue of compromise: they make a virtue of taking their time. "Hot potatoes", they say, "should be put in the refrigerator." The hope is that further reflection and investigation, as well as cooling tempers, will yield the very compromise that initially proved elusive. Some issues in the event prove evanescent and simply go away. Others are handed over to independent commissions and other forms of public inquiry for further consideration. Needless to say, such commissions and inquiries usually take months, even years, to report. In Dutch politicians' eyes, that is precisely the point. Few issues are *really* urgent: why treat almost every issue as though it were?

If one way of dealing with hot political issues is to put them in the refrigerator, another is to have a go at taking them out of politics. In some countries, the dominant urge of most politicians is to politicise each and every issue that arises, to make it, almost whatever it is, the subject of party-political controversy. Vigorous contestation is the name of the game, and the game is always being played. It goes without saying that Dutch politicians also hold strong views and are perfectly capable of engaging in vigorous controversy; but if an issue shows signs of becoming too divisive, of inflaming passions to the point where they may cause serious harm, the Dutch instinct is to attempt to remove the issue altogether from the political arena. This is yet another service performed by the Netherlands' endless commissions and enquiries. One advantage from the Dutch point of view of their country's membership of the European Union is that issues that are to too hot for them to handle on their own can, with luck, be handled successfully in the wider European context.

A third way the Dutch have of dealing with hot political potatoes is not really a method or a technique: it is more a faith: a faith in "the facts" and, by extension, a faith in disinterested academic research and disinterested expert advice. When the Dutch hand over a problem to an independent commission, they are not merely (to use the English expression) kicking the ball into touch, though they may well be doing that: they are also, and genuinely, seeking to take advantage of the commission's expertise and knowledge. "Don't confuse me with the facts" is not a phrase that would ever occur to a Dutch politician or civil servant. In the view of the Dutch, seemingly intractable questions of value often dissolve in the light of new factual knowledge and understanding. The Dutch approach is to try, wherever possible, to reduce the emotional to the technical, the high-flown to the mundane. This approach, in the Netherlands, is often remarkably successful.

IV

It will already be clear to the reader—there is no need to labour the point—that Dutch democracy and the Dutch constitution conform remarkably closely to the first of our two archetypes, the power-sharing archetype. Indeed it deviates from that model in only two respects. In the first place, the Dutch system is very highly centralised in the geographical sense; both local and provincial government in the Netherlands is weak. In the second place, the courts play a much more limited role than they do in countries such as France, Germany and the United States. Specifically, the Dutch courts are precluded by the terms of the Dutch capital-C Constitution from declaring acts of the Dutch parliament unconstitutional. (As may be inferred, although the Dutch do have a capital-C Constitution, they do not take it desperately seriously. They amend it easily and often.)

One consequence of the laborious Dutch mode of policy making should be noted. It is one predicted by the power-sharing archetype. It is that, once policy has finally been determined in the Netherlands, it almost at once gains broad acceptance both among the political class and among the population at large. Once an issue, no matter how emotional and controversial an issue, has been settled, it stays settled. Changes of public policy are rare; threats to abandon existing lines of policy or to repeal existing legislation are almost unknown. Governments in the Netherlands seldom or never make U-turns; changes of government seldom presage major changes of policy. As a result, the overall pattern of policy in the Netherlands remains remarkably stable. It is as though the very labour of making policy in the Dutch system is so wearisome that, once a policy has been agreed upon, no one any longer has the stomach for further debate and negotiation. "Whew", the Dutch people seem collectively to say, "we've had enough of that. Let's move on."

This is not the place to offer a detailed explanation of why the Dutch system in its present form exists and why it works in the way that it does; the short answer is that the Dutch system embodies in present-day institutional structures and cultural norms the successful efforts made by Dutch politicians several generations ago to find ways of accommodating the deep political and religious divisions that at that time threatened to rend the Dutch nation. Rather, what matters from our point of view is not why the Dutch system developed as it did but the simple, elemental fact that it does work as it does—and, moreover, that it works extremely well. It is an extremely successful example of the power-sharing archetype.

More specifically, the Dutch system does not seize up in the Netherlands' rare moments of national crisis. Government policy in the Netherlands seems about as robust and coherent as anybody else's. The Dutch system *is* somewhat cumbrous and slow-moving, but the delays inherent in the policy-making processes just described do not seem to do any particular harm and probably do some good. Perhaps most remarkable of all is the fact that the Dutch system, which might be expected to suffer from immobility amounting to stasis, is in fact, by world standards, highly innovative. The Dutch have in effect legalised the use of a range of drugs in addition to alcohol. They have made euthanasia legally available under some circumstances. They have given legal recognition to stable relationships between gay women and men. Whether or not one approves of these particular innovations, they are hardly signs of a system that is paralysed. As it happens, the Dutch are also among the richest people in the world, with the highest standards of education, health, transport and other public services. The Dutch system does work.

Moreover, despite the oddly limited role that elections play in Dutch politics and despite the fact that most of the endless negotiations that characterise Dutch political life take place in secret, behind closed doors, all of the available evidence indicates that the Dutch quite like their system. They approve of it. They show no signs of wishing to change it. To take just one example, the Eurobarometer studies funded by the European Commission regularly ask representative samples of the peoples of every EU member country: "On the whole, are you very satisfied, fairly satisfied, not very satisfied or not at all satisfied with the way democracy works in [your country]?" The Eurobarometer findings consistently show that the Dutch are among the most satisfied of any people in Europe with their version of liberal democracy. They are far more satisfied than the peoples of, for example, France and the United Kingdom.[6]

So the Dutch system is a power-sharing system, and it is also a successful system, almost no matter how the "success" of a polity is measured. However, the purpose of examining the Dutch system has not been for its own sake, because we are particularly interested in the Netherlands as a country. It has been, rather, to put down a marker, to provide a benchmark in the form of a nearly pure power-sharing system against which a largely power-hoarding system can be compared.

The reader will not be surprised to be told that our chosen example of a power-hoarding system is that of the United Kingdom. In the next chapter, we deal with the way in which democracy in the United Kingdom has traditionally functioned and has been traditionally understood. The United Kingdom and the Netherlands could scarcely differ more.

2. THE BRITISH TRADITION AND ITS LOGIC

Coriolanus, as many readers will know, is one of the most political of Shakespeare's many political plays, as well as being one of the most arresting psychologically. One of the play's principal political themes is the relationship in ancient Rome between governors and governed and, in particular, the relationship between Caius Martius—as Coriolanus was known before acquiring his flashy title—and the common people of Rome. Caius Martius is a man of great physical courage, valiant in battle, but he is also arrogant, tactless and stubborn. Much of the play turns on Caius Martius' refusal to accede to the Roman plebeians' increasingly vociferous political demands.

At one point in the action—the specific context does not matter—Caius Martius says this:

> [The people] said they were an-hungry, sighed forth proverbs—
> That hunger broke stone walls, that dogs must eat,
> That meat was made for mouths, that the gods sent not
> Corn for the rich men only. With these shreds
> They vented their complainings; which being answered
> And a petition granted them—a strange one,
> To break the heart of generosity
> And make bold power look pale—they threw their caps
> As they would hang them on the horns o' th' moon,
> Shouting their emulation.

His friend Menenius interrupts to ask: "What is granted them?" To which Caius Martius replies:

> Five tribunes to defend their vulgar wisdoms,
> Of their own choice. One's Junius Brutus, one
> Sicinius Velutus, and—I know not. S'death!
> The rabble should have first unroofed the city
> Ere so prevailed with me.[1]

Two points about this simple-sounding passage are worth noting. Both illustrate aspects of the British political tradition—

as one might expect from Shakespeare—and we shall come back to them.

The first is that, even though the common people of Rome are granted their petition, to Caius Martius' extreme irritation, there is no suggestion in *Coriolanus* that the Roman people were actually seeking to *become* the government of the city. It is assumed by Caius Martius, by the common people and by the playwright himself that there will continue to be, on the one hand, the governors of Rome, in the form of the Senate, and, on the other hand, the governed of Rome, in the form of the mass of the common people. The issue is not whether the Roman people are to take over the government and become one with it but, rather, how the continuing relationships between these two entities—government and people—are to be regulated. As we have seen, Caius Martius takes one view; the people and an admittedly reluctant Senate take another.

The second point, closely related, is that the common people, while not seeking to take over the government, are nevertheless to be allowed to bring their influence directly to bear upon it. They are to have "five tribunes, to defend their vulgar wisdoms". The people's influence on the government is to come from outside the government, but they *are* to have influence—and, more than that, a formal, institutionalised means of exercising that influence. Here is one way—one with a long and distinguished pedigree—of conceiving of the proper relationship between governors and governed in a constitutional order. The governors govern. The people have their say.

It is against that background that we turn, at last, to consider the United Kingdom's traditional constitution. Note the word "traditional". In this chapter, we are dealing, not entirely but to a large extent, with the past. How far the past lives on in the present we shall consider in Chapter 4.

II

The salient features of the traditional UK constitution were as follows. Taken as a whole, they correspond almost perfectly with the power-hoarding archetype described in Chapter 1.

By the early years of the 20th century, the United Kingdom, although still a monarchy in form, had become virtually a republic in fact. The king or queen had over time surrendered all real political power. He or she had become an adornment of the state rather than an essential part of it, a wreath-layer and road-opener rather than in any sense a decision maker. To be sure, the king or queen popped up from time to time at moments of political crisis, such as that over the House of Lords in 1909–11 or when Ramsay MacDonald's Labour Government broke up in 1931; but such moments were exceedingly rare and become more so as time went on. Moreover, even when a crisis did occur, the monarch's role was restricted to that of neutral arbiter or honest broker, the same role as that played by figurehead presidents in many parliamentary regimes such as the German and the Italian. In this respect, though in few others, the British system resembles that of the Netherlands, where the queen (the Dutch have not had a king since 1890) does play a modest brokerage role in connection with the formation of new coalition governments but is otherwise politically impotent.

The courts, too, were not an autonomous source of political power under the traditional British constitution. The courts were important, of course, as they are in every properly functioning constitutional system. British judges' independence of both the government and Parliament, and their insistence that the state as well as its citizens should be subject to the law, were and are essential bulwarks of good government. Compared, however, with the role of the courts in many other countries, the role of the courts in the United Kingdom was severely circumscribed. Judges might occasionally be said to have "made policy" as a result of their individual decisions or series of decisions, but they could not declare Acts of Parliament unconstitutional because there was no capital-C Constitution in Britain, and they could not determine that Acts of Parliament or acts of the government were in breach of the bill of rights because there was no bill of rights. As a result, few British judges became famous, and those who did tended to achieve notoriety for their personal eccentricities or their outrageous slurs on women and racial minorities rather than their legal rulings. The UK courts had nowhere near the political clout of the US Supreme Court, the German Constitutional Court or the French *Conseil d'Etat*. It is striking that college textbooks on British government and politics published in the 20th century almost never devoted a separate chapter to the judiciary. A textbook on American government without a chapter on the Supreme Court and the political role of the US judiciary would be inconceivable.

Under Britain's traditional constitution, there was also no autonomous or quasi-autonomous tier of regional, state or provincial government. Not only was the system not federal in the manner of the German, Canadian or American systems, but there was no subnational regional tier of government such as those that the French and Italians developed in the 1970s.

Scotland preserved its national systems of education and criminal and civil law, and the Scottish Office in Edinburgh, under a fully fledged Secretary of State for Scotland from 1926 onwards, enjoyed a substantial degree of administrative autonomy; but Scotland otherwise had no distinct political existence and all Acts of Parliament affecting Scotland (even if they affected exclusively Scotland) were Acts of the United Kingdom Parliament—as though California were governed in every respect from Washington DC.

Wales was to an even greater extent a satrapy of London. Although the Principality acquired its own Secretary of State in 1964, his powers were limited, and when the Conservative Party was in power after 1979 the Secretary of State for Wales was frequently not even a Welshman or the representative of a Welsh constituency. The only exception to this general pattern was Northern Ireland, where the Stormont Parliament and the Northern Ireland government (under someone actually called "Prime Minister of Northern Ireland") enjoyed almost total local autonomy from 1922 until the reimposition of direct rule from Westminster in 1972. The phrase "direct rule" is telling. Scotland and Wales were directly ruled from London all along.

The point made in the last paragraph needs, however, to be qualified in one important particular. Although Britain lacked a regional or provincial tier of government, it did possess a well-developed local tier of government, and for most of the last century local authorities in England, Scotland, Wales and Northern Ireland enjoyed a substantial measure of local autonomy. Local authorities in the UK were the legal creatures of central government, which could create them, abolish them or reorganise them at will; their capital expenditures were strictly controlled from the centre; and they were further constrained by the *ultra vires* rule, which stipulated that they could do only what Parliament expressly permitted or enjoined them to do. In other words, what was not expressly permitted them was expressly forbidden. Nevertheless, despite these constraints and despite their formal subordination to the centre, UK local authorities were held on only a loose rein by most Whitehall departments. With its long history and its rich accretion of local interests and traditions, local government in the UK was, for all practical purposes, an essential element of the traditional UK constitution.

Education provided a good example. Popularly elected local education authorities—local councils under another guise—built schools, hired teachers and, together with the teaching profession, determined the curriculum. Education in the UK was a locally provided service; the centre seldom intervened. The famous Butler Education Act of 1944—named after R.A. Butler, the Education Minister in Churchill's wartime coalition—simply took it for granted that education at the primary, secondary and further levels would be a local responsibility. The Act's first clause did refer to the local education authorities' acting under the Minister of Education's "control and direction", but in practice there was, initially, precious little control and not much more direction. The Act and the Ministry of Education even left local education authorities largely free to organise their own school systems along academic lines as they saw fit. For example, those responsible for the passage of the Act envisaged a tripartite division of secondary schools into grammar, technical and secondary modern, but, beginning in the late 1940s and 1950s, a number of local education authorities across England and Wales, some Conservative-controlled, began to experiment with so-called "comprehensive" schools. They were entirely free to do so.

Moreover, over a period of many decades the largely autonomous world of local government tended to expand rather than contract. As the role of the state in general expanded, so did the role of these local statelets. Local authorities provided their citizens not only with education but also with trams and buses, municipal baths and sports facilities, housing on a vast scale, public libraries, museums and art galleries, a wide variety of personal social services and much else besides. Famously, the city of Hull for many years provided the local telephone service. The locally generated revenues of local authorities in England, Scotland and Wales rose from £273 million shortly after the end of the Second World War to £1,557 million a quarter of a century later. Their expenditures during the same period rose from £711 million to £4,392 million.[2] Part of the increase was accounted for by inflation, but most was not. In terms of both their independence of Whitehall and the scope of their activities, the twenty-five years after the war constituted something of a golden age for local authorities in this country.

If, however, local government did for a long period constitute a quasi-autonomous source of political power in the British system, the civil service, despite the claims sometimes made on its behalf, most certainly did not. To be sure, senior civil servants in the postwar period were confident in both themselves and their judgments, and a few individuals—Sir Frank Lee and Dame Evelyn Sharp were famous examples—did exert considerable influence on policy. Civil servants during that era saw themselves as governing the country not at the behest of ministers but in active collaboration with them. In departments with stupid, idle or passive ministers (of whom, admittedly, there were always many in Whitehall), officials almost invariably took charge; they had no option. In addition, a few departments, notably the Treasury, the Home Office and the Board of Trade, pursued what amounted to independent departmental policies, which it was extremely difficult for all but the most determined ministers to change.

But, for all that, the British civil service was never quite an estate of the realm. Unlike the French civil service, it never developed a vivid sense of itself as a group of men with a mission to preserve and promote national security and grandeur. Nor did the British civil service, whether individually or collectively, have a self-defined policy mission. Few individual civil servants, let alone the whole civil service, had substantive policy goals which they were prepared, if necessary, to pursue even in the face of ministerial opposition. The overwhelming majority of British civil servants accepted that in the end they were just that: servants, of the Crown in theory, of the passing parade of ministers in practice. It was a badge of honour (to cite a famous example) to nationalise the UK steel industry under Attlee, to denationalise it under Churchill and to renationalise it under Wilson. The same officials, had they lived long enough, would have re-denationalised it under Thatcher. Sir Robert Armstrong was merely articulating existing practice when he wrote in 1985:

> Civil servants are servants of the Crown. For all practical purposes the Crown in this context means and is represented by the Government of the day . . . The Civil Service as such has no constitutional personality or responsibility separate from the duly elected Government of the day.[3]

The position of interest groups in the traditional constitution was more complicated. A few of them, of course, possessed brute social power. That is, they controlled goods that both state and nation required and, in addition, from time to time were willing and able to withdraw or withhold those goods. If the miners struck, to take the most extreme case, the lights went out. Most groups, however, either did not possess such goods or, even if they did possess them, were unwilling or unable to take full advantage of the fact. Doctors would not strike; farmers could not (though they could, and in a later age did, disrupt). Nevertheless, even when brute social power was not at issue, ministers and officials knew that they needed much of what the groups had to offer: essential information, advice, goodwill, a degree of passive consent, on many occasions active cooperation. The medical profession was not powerful in the way that the miners were; but the Ministry of Health listened to the British Medical Association all the same. The farmers were likewise not powerful (though many politicians feared their votes); but it was widely supposed that the Ministry of Agriculture had actually been colonised by the National Farmers' Union. Interest groups were listened to, and there certainly existed under the traditional constitution all manner of contacts between the groups and the government, contacts that ranged from the wholly informal but frequently intimate to the more formal and institutionalised. As in the Netherlands, advisory groups of one sort or another abounded.

Interestingly, however, the British never developed what might be called, rather pretentiously, a doctrine of the proper role of interest groups. On the one hand, the groups were acknowledged, accepted and in many cases befriended; on the other hand, they were always regarded as ultimately external, other: they were never fully assimilated into the state. During some periods, notably during the Second World War and for a time during the 1960s, the relationships between the groups and the government become so close and intertwined that commentators began to speak of nascent corporatism in the UK. During other periods, however, notably during the premiership of Margaret Thatcher in the 1980s, organised interests were regarded as virtually enemies of the state; Thatcher had as little to do with the groups as she could, kept them at arm's length and invited her ministers to do the same. In so far as there was a relevant doctrine, it included the belief, among all parties, including the groups themselves, that the government had its duties, that the groups had theirs, that each side should act on its own responsibilities and that the two sides should never become *too* close. In many quarters, the extreme intimacy of the relations between the Ministry of Agriculture and the NFU, and between the Ministry of Education and the teachers' unions, was viewed with more than a touch of disapproval.

The role of Parliament in the traditional British system was exceedingly circumscribed. In practice, parliamentary sovereignty meant government-of-the-day sovereignty. Members of the House of Commons on the government side could and did bring pressure to bear on ministers, especially at times when the government's majority in the House was small; and opposition MPs, for their part, could harry ministers, deprive them of much-needed sleep and sometimes effectively obstruct their parliamentary business. In addition, no prime minister could ever afford to lose sight of the fact that in the end he held his lofty position, not in his own right, but in his role as leader of the majority party in the House of Commons. The MPs of his party chose him; they could in principle un-choose him (though in practice they almost never did). The dialogue between ministers and backbenchers on the government side was continuous, and ministers quite often yielded to backbench pressure or more often, by anticipating it, ensured that it was not applied in the first place. The House of Commons under the traditional constitution was far from totally impotent.

But, that said, it was a pretty feeble institution most of the time, certainly as compared with parliaments in many other countries, not to mention the United States Congress. Party discipline was tight, and almost all votes were whipped votes; governments seldom lived in fear of their parliamentary lives. It further strengthened the government's position that, although there were always a few mavericks, the great majority of government backbenchers believed it was their duty to sustain the government—the government of *their* party—in office. Members' professional self-definition, as well as concern for their own political survival, precluded them from seeking to organise as any kind of effective counterweight to the government. As individual MPs, many backbenchers did want to join the government, but that was precisely because they knew that they were not already a part of it. The House of Common was not a governing institution, and few, if any, MPs imagined that it was.

The culture of the place and party discipline apart, the House of Commons' rules also guaranteed, or virtually guaranteed, parliamentary subservience. The government controlled the parliamentary timetable. Ministers, and only ministers, could propose legislation raising revenue or entailing substantial amounts of government expenditure. The government, with the support of its backbenchers, could cut short parliamentary debate by means of the guillotine. The House of Commons' Standing Committees, usually government-dominated, were recruited on a non-specialist basis, lacked staff and also lacked the power to hold hearings and summon witnesses who could be questioned on the merits of proposed legislation. The so-called Select Committees did tend to attract MPs with specialist knowledge, they did have limited staff, and they could hold hearings and summon witnesses; but ministers and officials were often unwilling fully to co-operate with their enquiries and, with rare exceptions, their eventual reports went largely unread. The reform of the Select Committee system introduced in 1979 under the aegis of Norman St John-Stevas certainly achieved far less than its supporters hoped for and its opponents feared. Not least, the government of the day not only controlled the parliamentary timetable: the government's legislative programme took up virtually the whole of that timetable. Members of Parliament who were not also ministers were restricted to asking questions, tabling motions and, if they happened to be lucky in an annual lottery, introducing Private Members' Bills (which, however, had a realistic chance of reaching the statute book only if they began with government support or else picked it up along the way). The term "Private Member" was hugely significant in itself. Non-ministerial members of the House of Commons were no more than Private Members: that is, in effect, private citizens with a certain public standing and certain powers and privileges but without any real share in the exercise of governmental power. The whole parliamentary opposition shared this lowly status.

The other house of Parliament, the House of Lords, once it had been stripped of its ultimate veto power by the Parliament Act 1911, and once the duration of its suspensory veto had been further reduced by the Parliament Act 1949, was neither here nor there. The body was Conservative-dominated. When a Conservative government was in power, the Lords almost invariably did the government's bidding. When a Labour government was in power, the Lords likewise almost invariably did the government's bidding, because they feared that, if they did not, their powers would be further reduced or they would be abolished altogether. The Lords were somewhat more likely to kick up a fuss when the Labour Party was in power, and they tended to make life more difficult for Labour than for Conservative ministers; but there was not much in it. Especially from the 1970s onwards, the unreformed House of Lords acquired something of a reputation for wisdom, probity and sound common sense—for being able to take the long view, for refusing to be blown about by the gusts of public opinion. But this reputation was largely self-generated. Significant Lords' interventions in the affairs of state attracted so much attention mostly because they were so rare.

What of the people? The people of the United Kingdom, as we shall see in a moment, played a crucial role in the traditional constitution—a role in many ways more crucial than the Dutch people's in their constitution—but the British people's role, like that of their Parliament, was severely circumscribed. In particular, the British people did not participate in any direct way in governmental decision making. There were no national referendums or plebiscites in the UK. And, moreover, there were not meant to be any—ever. No feature of British political doctrine was more deeply entrenched under the traditional constitution than the belief that the people should not take policy decisions: the politicians, and the politicians alone, should take them. As in ancient Rome, there were governors and governed in traditional Britain, and the roles of the two were never to be confused. The people were *not* to govern themselves. In L.S. Amery's classic postwar formulation: "Our system is one of democracy, but of democracy by consent and not by delegation, of government of the people, for the people, with, but not by, the people."[4]

The idea of referendums, as already indicated, was considered to be peculiarly repugnant. Early in the last century Lord Loreburn, the then Liberal Lord Chancellor, was adamant in opposing a proposed referendum on the future of the House of Lords:

> The referendum would . . . be fatal to representative government. The political genius of the English people was the first to discover, and after great difficulty to develop, the real basis of liberty and of self-government in this country—a system which has been copied all over the world. Every referendum is an attack on the representative system.[5]

Nearly half a century later, Clement Attlee in 1945 rejected with horror the suggestion that a referendum might be held on whether or not the wartime coalition should continue in office:

> I could not consent to the introduction into our national life of a device so alien to all our traditions as the referendum, which has only too often been the instrument of Nazism and Fascism. Hitler's practices in the field of referenda and plebiscites can hardly have endeared these expedients to the British heart.[6]

Similar sentiments were expressed during the great Common Market debates of the early 1970s. The people were to be kept in their appointed place. Caius Martius would have approved.

To sum up: local government enjoyed substantial autonomy and power under Britain's traditional political arrangements, but there were few other institutions that did. The Monarchy as a power base had faded away. The courts remained independent but had little political clout. There was no regional or provincial tier of government. The civil service played an important but ultimately subservient role. Interest groups occupied an anomalous intermediate position, partly inside the government machine but mainly outside it. Despite its ancient glories and vaunted reputation, the UK Parliament could not be counted among the world's more influential legislatures. The British people themselves were excluded from decision making, at least from direct decision making. In short, the traditional system in the UK—in conformity with the power-hoarding archetype—boasted few sources of political power that were both autonomous, capable of acting on their own, and at the same time legitimate.

III

It did, however, boast some such sources. The United Kingdom was far from being a dictatorship. Thus far, we have focussed on, so to speak, negatives and absences—on what the traditional British constitution did *not* comprise. It is time now to turn to positives and presences—to what it *did* comprise. Like a great Gothic cathedral, the traditional British constitution was in some ways immensely subtle and complicated, having evolved slowly over centuries and bearing mute witness to the full complexity of real-world political life; but, also like a Gothic cathedral, its ground plan was in fact very simple. If one did not allow one's eye to be distracted by the innumerable gargoyles and bosses, one could easily discern the building's basic shape.

Its principal feature was, of course, the government. The government predated all the rest. It took the form initially of the king, then of the king and his ministers, then of his ministers and the king, then of his ministers (for all practical purposes) without the king. The government was where authority in the British system lay. It was also where it was concentrated. All those who aspired to political power in Britain aspired to be members of the government; they did not aspire to be judges or mayors or civil servants or the chairs of House of Commons Select Committees. The government possessed a wide range of prerogative powers, inherited from the Crown. All important legislation was government legislation. The government was in sole control of the national budget, on both the revenue and the expenditure sides. It was also in sole control of Britain's relations with other countries. If there was a national problem to be solved or a national crisis to be faced, everyone in the land looked to the government of the day to take the lead. The government was *the* pro-active element in the British system. Everyone else, and everything else, was essentially reactive, responding to initiatives rather than taking them. The British system, by no means uniquely in the world but in an extreme form, was a government-centred system.

The details of who held power within the government need not detain us here. Suffice it to say that, while the system remained throughout a nominally collegial system, with power centred in the cabinet, the actual practices of governments varied widely. Campbell-Bannerman and Asquith were followed by Lloyd George. Baldwin was followed by the far more imperious Chamberlain. Churchill was followed by Attlee, Macmillan by Douglas-Home. And so on. In some governments, the prime minister was wholly dominant. In others, such as Attlee's after the war, power was shared among the prime minister and three or four powerful barons. In yet others, the prime minister was more chairman and referee than, in any real sense, a political leader. The notion that the British system has become inexorably more "prime ministerial" is hard to sustain in the light of the historical evidence.

The other principal element in the traditional constitution, once the UK had entered its democratic phase, was the people, also known as the electorate. The people were not to govern, but they were to be assigned the immensely important task of choosing the government. The ancient Romans elected "five tribunes to defend their vulgar wisdoms"; modern Britons elected their equivalent of the whole Roman Senate. The electorate grew by nearly half at the time of the 1832 Great Reform Act. It then grew by 88 per cent as a result of the franchise extension of 1867 and by 67 per cent as a result of the franchise extension of 1885.[7] Finally, between the turn of the last century and the late 1920s, it increased no less than fourfold as a result of the coming of universal adult suffrage.[8] Britain was not really a fully fledged democracy until the 1920s, but after that it most assuredly was.

The instruments of the people's will in the United Kingdom were two political parties, initially the Conservatives and Liberals, then from the late 1920s onwards the Conservatives and Labour. At every general election, the voters had a simple dichotomous choice: one major party or the other, up or down, in or out. Minor parties existed, of course, but they attracted little support. Voters knew that votes cast for the minor parties were wasted votes—wasted in the sense of not being effective in helping to elect the government. Between 1931 and 1970, once the two-party system had re-established itself after the demise of the Liberals, the Conservative and Labour parties between them never secured less than 85 per cent of the popular vote and frequently secured well over 90 per cent. No one in Britain could be in any doubt who the real contenders for power were.

The British party system had another important property: it was a national system. There were, of course, large numbers of individual constituencies in which one or other of the two main parties predominated. Nevertheless, both of the main parties competed nationwide. The major electoral contenders in England were the Conservatives and Labour. The major electoral contenders in Scotland were the Conservatives and Labour (though the Scottish Conservatives preferred to call themselves Unionists). The major electoral contenders in Wales were also the Conservatives and Labour. Only in Northern Ireland was there substantial deviation. The Conservatives did compete, as Unionists, in Northern Ireland elections, but the London-based Labour Party did not. The political space in Northern Ireland left vacant by Labour's absence was filled by a number of smaller parties, most of them, though not all, Nationalist and Republican. The national character of the two-party system meant that the whole of the United Kingdom apart from Northern Ireland constituted—in effect, though not in form—a single political constituency. Great Britain, in that sense, was one nation.

The existence of two and only two major parties in the UK was no accident; nor did it represent a spontaneous welling up of popular sentiment from, as it were, two vents in the ocean floor. A crucial feature of Britain's traditional constitutional arrangements was the simple plurality first-past-the-post electoral system. The system, as it actually operated, had two significant effects. One was to reduce to two the number of political parties seriously contending for power. The other was to make it highly probable that whichever party won a plurality of votes at a general election would also win an absolute majority of seats in the House of Commons. The system also made it likely—no more than that—that one of the two major parties would win an absolute majority of seats in the Commons even if it did not succeed in winning a plurality of votes. Between 1931 and 1970 there were ten general elections, and either the Conservatives or Labour won an overall Commons majority at every one of them. In nine of the ten cases, the party winning the most votes also won the most seats. In the tenth, the general election of 1951, Labour won fractionally more votes than the Conservatives but the Conservatives nevertheless secured a majority in Parliament.

And that was basically it. There were two major political parties. They competed nationally. The people went to the polls every few years to choose between them. The party that won the most seats in the House of Commons invariably won an absolute majority of those seats. That party thereupon formed a government, with its leader as prime minister. The government governed. The opposition opposed. The people, having given voice to their "vulgar wisdoms", duly went home and remained there for another few years. The link between the act of voting and the act of government-formation in the United Kingdom, unlike in the Netherlands, was completely straightforward.

These institutional arrangements were accompanied, hardly surprisingly, by what might be called a culture of contestation. Occasionally the leaders of the two major parties co-operated, notably during the First and Second World Wars (though not during the Boer War), and they were occasionally prepared to negotiate an inter-party truce on a specific issue, for example over the future of Northern Ireland during most of the period following the reimposition of direct rule in 1972. But such co-operation was not only rare: it was regarded as highly anomalous. The true spirit of the British system was summed up in the exultant phrase of the newly elected Labour MP Sir Hartley Shawcross in 1945: "We are the masters now!" On the same occasion, a number of Labour MPs, as though to fix the moral and political distance that they saw separating themselves from the defeated Conservatives, sang "The Red Flag" in the House of Commons chamber.

British politicians' reluctance to co-operate extended to a more generalised reluctance to seek agreement on policy or anything else. Agreement often occurred, but it was seldom actively sought; and, even when it was actively sought, it tended to be sought surreptitiously—"behind the Speaker's chair"—as though the participants were somewhat ashamed to be seen doing business together. Consensus-seeking marked, and marks, the Dutch system; dissensus-seeking marked, and marks, the British system. If disagreements did not exist, they should be invented. If they did exist, as they usually did, they should be exploited. A striking manifestation of this urge to dispute was the tendency of all political issues in Britain to become politicised in the sense of becoming the subject of party-political controversy. Each of the two major parties had to have policies on everything, and it was unthinkable that the two parties' policies should be allowed to appear to resemble each other too closely. To the British television viewer or radio listener, it always came as a shock when spokesmen for the two major parties admitted openly that they agreed with one another. It seldom happened.

A reluctance to co-operate and to seek points of agreement implies great confidence in the correctness of one's own point of view; and those who are confident in their own point of view, or wish to appear confident, are also liable to be extremely reluctant to compromise. A hurrah word in Dutch politics, "compromise" has always been a boo word in British politics, even though, of course, compromises are essential and take place all the time. Another, newer term of opprobrium was the U-turn. Governments and parties were not only supposed to have policies on everything: they were supposed to stick to their policies even when they proved to be ill-advised or impracticable. In a curious way, rigidity came in Britain to be seen as a virtue, flexibility as a vice.

The single party, government-centred nature of the British system also had the effect of making it difficult—not impossible, but difficult—to put hot potatoes in the refrigerator. Royal Commissions could always be, and sometimes were, sent away to take evidence and meditate on intractable issues or ones that the government preferred not to take immediate responsibility for, and there were all kinds of government-appointed commissions and committees of enquiry. But, nevertheless, there was always pressure on British governments—from the media, from the opposition and often from the public—to respond instantly to new situations and concerns; and ministers often seemed anxious, even eager, to respond to this pressure in the shortest possible time. It was almost as though ministers positively enjoyed being over-tired and frantic. Governments of all parties seemed to adopt as their operating principle Churchill's famous injunction "Action this day!". If they failed to take immediate action on a particular issue and said instead "We had better go away and think about it", they could count on being given a hard time by their opponents.

Needless to say, winner take all, the political norm in the UK, also precluded any hint of the Dutch practice of proportionality. Members of the main opposition party were appointed as a matter of routine to high-profile public bodies like the BBC Board of Governors, and after 1973 one of Britain's two EU commissioners was always a member of the opposition; but, as a general rule, public appointments were made either on a non-partisan basis or on a partisan basis heavily biased in favour of the party in power. Mayors in Britain were never appointed from the centre as they are in the Netherlands, but, if they had been, it is impossible to imagine that Labour governments would have appointed known Conservatives to be mayors of Exeter or Leeds or that Conservative governments would have appointed known Labour supporters to preside over Manchester or Liverpool. The lay magistracy was the only major British institution in which the principle of proportionality, or at least of sharing out, was quite strictly applied.

This, in outline, was the traditional British system. It certainly conformed broadly to our power-hoarding archetype. It failed to conform to it in only two important respects. In the first place, local government in Britain constituted an autonomous centre of political power to a greater extent than allowed for by the archetype; central government for many decades effectively shared power with Britain's local authorities. And, secondly, the more important interest groups were always quite close to government and from time to time became virtually part of it, phases of arm's length alternating with phases of close embrace. But otherwise political power in the UK was both highly concentrated and almost completely centralised.

The picture painted of Britain's power-hoarding regime should not be too harsh. Despite the culture of contestation, common membership of the House of Commons created a certain camaraderie among Britain's top politicians, and friendships across party lines were far from unknown. Deals on occasion could be done, and were. In addition, if the two major parties were divided by the desire of each to displace the other in office, they were united during most of the 20th century by a consciousness that, if they were to displace the other party in office, they had to appeal, at least in part, to the other party's voters. Most British voters, including the supporters of both major parties, held middling or moderate views. Both of the two major parties therefore had to appeal to voters with middling or moderate views. Inevitably, as a result, the parties' policy positions and their general approach to politics also tended to be middling or moderate. Foreign observers of British politics noted the absence in Britain of both extreme left-wing communist parties and extreme right-wing fascist parties.

The picture painted of the traditional British system should also not give the impression that the governing of Britain was an especially easy task. Power hoarded is not necessarily power easy to wield. The pressures on the power-holders, *i.e.* the government, were almost invariably severe, with every one of the country's problems forced to flow through a single narrow channel. Dutch politicians are able to share the burdens of power and thereby lighten them. Political leaders in the UK had no such option. The intense competition of British political life, and the culture of contestation itself, still further intensified the pressures under which Britain's politicians laboured. Labour ministers during the 1947 fuel crisis or Conservative ministers during the 1956 Suez crisis must often have wondered how many real advantages their putative power accorded them.

IV

As must be evident, Britain's power-hoarding constitution lacked American-style checks and balances. Americans, even American admirers of Britain, often described it as an "unbalanced constitution". But what was its internal logic? What were the underlying principles according to which it could be justified and defended?

It must be said straightaway that there were a number of principles according to which it could *not* be justified. Certainly no serious attempt was ever made to justify it in these terms. The fact that the British constitution had grown up piecemeal over time, that there had never been a defining "constitutional moment" in the UK, analogous to the Philadelphia convention of 1787 or the debates that led to Germany's Basic Law in 1949, meant that the British had never had to address themselves to the question of what purposes their constitution was meant to serve. Probably for that reason, they never seemed to notice that there were certain purposes that their constitution was not serving. The UK constitution was just there, given, a fact of life.

One of the principal givens of the old constitution was the one that restricted the electorate's role to that of voting every four or five years. No referendums. No plebiscites. No town meetings. No elaborate processes of public consultation. The government continued to govern just as it had in pre-democratic days. Not only that, but governments in the UK felt under no real obligation to pay any attention to public opinion. They might pay attention to public opinion on grounds of prudence—that is, if they were afraid of losing the next election. But they felt under no *moral* obligation to attend to the general public's wishes. Indeed they felt under a moral obligation *not* to listen to the public's views if what they heard was, in their view, misguided or in error. Edmund Burke's 18th-century remarks about being in unreserved communication with his constituents but refusing to sacrifice to them either his mature judgment or his enlightened conscience were much quoted, and with approval. Opponents of capital punishment, in parliamentary debates on the subject, frequently acknowledged that a majority in the country remained in favour of hanging but took the view that it was their right, and their duty, as MPs to vote the other way. More recently, it cut remarkably little ice in the debates on Scottish devolution that the people of Scotland actually appeared to *want* devolution. In the British tradition, the voice of the people, far from being the voice of God, was a mere clamour, which it might or might not be prudent to listen to on any particular occasion.

Thus, the traditional constitution could not be justified on grounds of pure democratic principle. Nor could it be justified on the ground that it maximised public involvement in politics. John Stuart Mill in *Considerations on Representative Government* maintained that representative government—or "popular government" as he called it—was desirable not only because it made for better government but also because it made for better citizens, better human beings. Democracy for him had a human as well as a political dimension. Active citizenship, he maintained, developed people's intellectual and moral capacities. It also encouraged them to take an active interest in their country and its welfare. "Let a person have nothing to do for his country", he wrote, "and he will not care for it."[9]

These views, however, were alien to the British political tradition, which emphasised government and the relationship between governors and governed rather than any concern for the moral well-being of the governed as such. Although the views of an eloquent Englishman, Mill's views never really found a resonance in his own country. The people of Britain were given the franchise during the 19th and 20th centuries, but they were then left free to do whatever they liked with it, including nothing. No moral or legal pressure was put on the British to vote. There were few American-style "get out the vote" campaigns. The notion of compulsory voting remained anathema. Partly as a result, the levels of turnout in UK elections, while perfectly respectable by United States standards, were consistently lower than in most countries on the European continent. The British people were given the chance to defend their vulgar wisdoms if they wanted to; but actually increasing those wisdoms, while it remained part of the educational agenda, was never part of Britain's political agenda.

Another ground on which the traditional constitution could not be, and was not, justified was the ground that it promoted national unity, that it increased the chances of the various peoples of the United Kingdom living in harmony together. The political arrangements of the Netherlands, as we noted briefly in the last chapter, arose out of fears in that country that, unless some means could be found of reconciling deep religious, economic and social divisions, the country might fall apart—or, more probably, be racked for generations by internal dissension. The British, however, did not fall prey to any such fears. They were confident in their national identity, confident in the cohesion of the United Kingdom and confident in the country's ultimate social cohesion. The traditional constitution did not address the question of national unity for the simple reason that the question did not arise.

This point is worth pausing over. People in this country are often amused by the quasi-reverence in which most Americans hold the capital-C Constitution of their country; be one of the US Constitution's provisions ever so absurd, many Americans will nevertheless brook no criticism of it. But, if one listened carefully, the traditional British constitution was often the subject of similar veneration. It was not written down. It was flexible. It had evolved through many generations. It embodied, therefore, the accumulated wisdom of the ages. And so forth. Sometimes the praise heaped upon our traditional constitution bordered on self-parody, as in this passage from a well-respected 19th-century historian:

> While the mechanical contrivances of political invention have crumbled away in the hands of their projectors, the goodly tree of British freedom, selecting from the kindly soil and assimilating its fit nutriment, still increases in stately bulk and still extends its unequalled development. Outliving the storms and vicissitudes of centuries, deeply rooted in the habits and affections of the people, it sheds far and wide its hospitable shade.[10]

That passage was quoted, without embarrassment, by a leading constitutional expert as recently as 1953.

The only difficulty with approaching the traditional constitution in that spirit is that it leaves something out. It suffers to a truly breathtaking extent from selective amnesia. There is one feature of modern British constitutional history that has been airbrushed out of Britain's collective memory almost as completely as the image of Trotsky was airbrushed out of Soviet-era photographs and films. In the years immediately following the First World War, the traditional British constitution failed its severest test. Ireland, or most of it, seceded. The United Kingdom fell apart. The British—though not the people of Northern Ireland—have conveniently forgotten this fact. Books on the British constitution typically fail even to mention it.

So far as one can tell, the majority of the people of Ireland—certainly the majority of Irish Catholics—were never desperately keen on being part of the United Kingdom. Daniel O'Connell in the 1820s had little trouble in organising the mass-membership Catholic Association to press, in the end successfully, for full Catholic emancipation. Agitation for the repeal of the Act of Union with Great Britain began in earnest in the 1840s, with hundreds of thousands of Irishmen taking part in orderly demonstrations. Following a period of relative quiescence in the aftermath of the Great Famine of that decade, the 1870s saw the rise of yet another mass movement, this time one in favour of home rule, or devolution, for Ireland. From the 1890s onwards, the Irish Nationalist Party, initially led by Charles Stewart Parnell, totally dominated Ireland's representation at Westminster, invariably with more than eighty MPs.

Successive British governments were aware of the scale of the discontent in Ireland. They could hardly not be. Sporadic efforts at repression and coercion were followed, beginning in the 1860s, with substantial measures of agrarian and ecclesiastical reform, many of them exceedingly radical by the standards of their day. But the issue of the constitutional relationship between Great Britain and Ireland, although it was addressed, was never settled. Gladstone introduced a Home Rule Bill in the House of Commons in 1886, but his party in Parliament split and it was decisively defeated. He introduced a second Home Rule Bill in 1893. This one passed the House of Commons but was defeated in the House of Lords. Asquith's government some twenty years later, in 1912, introduced yet another Home Rule Bill, the third. On this occasion, amidst increasingly violent resistance to home rule among Unionists, chiefly in the north, the Bill was passed into law, but implementation of the new legislation was suspended when war broke out at the beginning of August 1914.

The sequel was dismal for anyone wanting to preserve the unity of the United Kingdom. Britain's failure to implement home rule, and the British army's brutality and incompetence following the 1916 Easter Rising, alienated thousands of hitherto loyal Irishmen who would, only a few years earlier, have been more than content with a substantial measure of devolution. At the 1918 UK general election, the old Irish Nationalist Party was all but wiped out, and Sinn Fein, committed to withdrawing completely from Westminster and establishing a separate Irish parliament, won almost every Irish seat outside Ulster. The Sinn Fein MPs duly refused to take their Westminster seats, British power and authority in most of the country rapidly crumbled, the Irish republicans established their own government and parliament in Dublin, and by 1922 Ireland, minus most of Ulster, was effectively independent. The UK had, in consequence, to be renamed, rather clumsily, the United Kingdom of Great Britain and *Northern* Ireland.

Moreover, although the separation of two peoples can sometimes take place peacefully, as in the case of Norway's 1905 separation from Sweden, Ireland's secession from the United Kingdom was exceedingly bloody, another fact that the British, though not the Irish, have conveniently forgotten. Estimates vary, but the number of deaths in the decade prior to Irish independence—British and Irish, republican and Unionist, military and civilian—cannot have been less than 1,800 and may have exceeded 2,100.[11] Ethnic cleansing took place on a formidable scale, with Catholic relief agencies estimating that between mid 1920 and mid 1922, in Belfast alone, some 23,000 Catholics were driven from their homes.[12]

In short, the traditional British constitution and those who operated it failed during the 19th and 20th centuries in what might be thought to have been their single most basic and elemental task: that of holding the country together and preventing its people from killing each other. Before 1922 the British constitution contained no Netherlands-like mechanisms for facilitating conciliation and harmony between the peoples of Britain and Ireland and between the two communities in Northern Ireland. After 1922, despite everything that had happened, it did not acquire any: the post-1922 Northern Ireland constitution, in particular, was simply a copy of the power-hoarding constitution of the United Kingdom. For what was clearly a failure of constitutional imagination, the people of Northern Ireland were to pay a heavy price.

V

If the traditional British constitution was not about popular self-rule or popular participation, and if it contained no provisions designed to maintain national unity, what *was* it about? How could it be defended and justified? The truth is that the traditional constitution, whatever its limitations, undoubtedly had certain solid strengths and a certain massive overall solidity. It was, in its way, a splendid constitution and was certainly widely admired. As its admirers never tired of pointing out, it survived for an extraordinarily long time.

One of its virtues was that it provided for stable government. Whereas in some countries administrations came and went, in Britain they tended to remain in office for considerable periods of time. Because there were only two parties, and because one of them usually won an overall majority in Parliament, the typical life of a British government was four or five years, and many governments lasted a good deal longer. Between the end of the Second World War and the mid 1990s, there were only five short periods of relative governmental instability: 1950-51, when the Attlee Government had only an exiguous majority and was subject to constant Conservative guerrilla raids in Parliament; 1964–66, when the first Wilson Government similarly had a small majority; February–October 1974, when the second Wilson Government had no majority at all; 1976–79, when the Callaghan Government had lost its majority and had to rely on Liberal support in Parliament; and the mid 1990s, when the Major Government often appeared to be in danger of being brought down, or at least thwarted, by its own nominal supporters. However, these *were* short-lived episodes: the norm in Britain was for long periods of stable government.

The contrast with some other countries was striking. In the early years of the French Fourth Republic, governments came and went with alarming frequency, and governmental instability was one of the principal causes of the collapse of that regime in 1958. To take another example, whereas Britain between the end of the war and the mid 1990s had 11 governments under ten prime ministers (Harold Wilson served twice), Italy during the same period had no fewer than 48 governments under 19 prime ministers. In Italy, the average government survived for less than a year; few survived for more than two years. Britons gazed across the Channel at France and Italy and were appalled by what they saw. (It has to be said that most Frenchmen and Italians were not greatly impressed either.)

That said, all was not quite as it seemed, and the Anglo-continental contrast could be overdone. In the first place, the comings and goings of French and Italian governments concealed a good deal of continuity of governing personnel. In Italy especially, the prime minister might change, and the composition of the governing coalition might change, but the same men (they were always men) often remained for many years in charge of key ministries such as Finance and Foreign Affairs. In Britain by contrast, the same prime minister and the same government might remain in office for a substantial period but with, at the same time, constant changes taking place among the holders of other principal offices. Between the late 1940s and the mid 1990s, there may have been only ten British prime ministers but there were 18 Chancellors of the Exchequer and 22 Foreign Secretaries. The cabinet reshuffle remained a British speciality.

In the second place, continuity of government by no means guarantees continuity of policy and discontinuity of government by no means guarantees discontinuity of policy. Stable government is not at all the same thing as a stable pattern of public policy. On the one hand, some of continental Europe's most unstable political systems in the postwar period nevertheless managed to maintain substantially stable policies, especially economic policies, over many years; the French Fourth Republic undoubtedly laid the foundations for the economic successes of the Fifth. On the other hand, British policy in many fields was marvellously changeable. Successive governments nationalised and denationalised, blew hot and cold on the UK's relationship with the Common Market and, during the 1970s and 1980s, changed the basis of trade union law with extraordinary frequency. Studies showed that British fiscal policy—both the structure of the tax system and the rates at which taxes were levied—varied more than that of any other advanced industrial country. Other countries' finance ministers may have come and gone, but British Chancellors of the Exchequer were uniquely fidgety.[13]

Thirdly, those who extolled the virtues of the British constitution as compared with those of other countries often chose their comparators rather selectively. They usually compared the UK with postwar France or Italy. They did not compare the UK nearly so often with other countries on the continent of Europe, such as Germany, the Netherlands and many of the Scandinavian countries, which, like France and Italy, also had proportional electoral systems and more than two major political parties but which nevertheless enjoyed considerable governmental and policy stability. Students of the British constitution were seldom in the business of sustained, systematic comparative enquiry.

Even so, governmental stability *was* a feature of the traditional British constitution and was also a virtue of it. British governments could plan further ahead than those in some other countries. They could sometimes effect radical changes in policy direction without having to fear immediate adverse consequences. The British people were almost certainly reassured by the fact that their governments were not constantly chopping and changing. Certainly many foreigners marvelled at the almost stately qualities that the British system exhibited.

Another virtue of the traditional constitution was that, on the whole, it made for moderate government. "Moderation" is a tricky concept, at least in politics. One person's moderation may be another person's extremism, and in any case moderation is not necessarily a virtue (during the war the British people would not have thanked Churchill if he had defended Britain "moderately"). But, if moderation is defined empirically as denoting situations in which, in a two-party system, the two major parties are not too far apart in terms of their policies and ideologies, then British politics during most of the 20th century was indeed moderate. Sometimes the leaders of the parties held not too dissimilar views; sometimes electoral considerations forced the parties close to each other. Either way, party conflict was damped down. Only during the 1970s and 1980s—when the Labour Party lurched to the left and the Conservative Party under Thatcher largely abandoned traditional Tory paternalism—was party competition in Britain not moderate in this empirical sense.

The traditional constitution thus provided the UK with moderate government (or at least was conducive to moderate government). It also, and perhaps more importantly, provided the UK with effective government. The system delivered. It worked. Governments were capable of taking decisions and implementing them. The number of veto points in the system was not so large as to make it easy to thwart almost any initiative for change. The gridlock so frequently found in other systems was largely avoided. Whatever else the United Kingdom was during most of the 20th century, it was a well-governed country compared with a large proportion of the world's other countries; and it was by no means absurd to link good government—as well as stable government—in Britain with the UK's power-hoarding type of constitution.

Again, however, a caveat needs to be entered. No one has ever undertaken a systematic study of the effectiveness of governments across a wide range of countries—a study that would have to define "effectiveness", find ways of measuring it and, in addition, find ways of linking effectiveness (or ineffectiveness) to other aspects of the political systems of the countries in question. It would, to say the least of it, be a formidable undertaking. If, however, such a study were undertaken, it is not entirely clear that the UK under its traditional constitution would necessarily have stood head and shoulders above most other liberal democracies. The British system, as we have just seen, was not especially effective in dealing with Ireland. A similar example might be trade union reform. It was clear to the leaders of both major parties as early as the mid 1960s that trade union reform was essential: reform of both the unions' internal structures and their relations with employers and the state. The same thing was also clear to most voters, including most trade union members. But the reform efforts of Labour in the 1960s, of the Conservatives in the 1970s and of Labour again in the 1970s were all failures, and it was not until the mid 1980s that effective reforms were finally put in place. A system that takes two decades to implement essential policy changes that have widespread public backing does not, on the face of it, appear to be a notably effective system.

But that is an aside. The effectiveness criterion is not an easy one to apply cross-nationally, and it is certainly the case that the traditional UK system was not desperately *in*effective in the way that the French system, for example, was before and immediately after the Second World War.

The three considerations so far mentioned—stability, moderation and effectiveness—have in common the fact that they are matters of contingency. The links between our traditional constitution and the British system's stability, moderation and effectiveness, if they existed at all, as they probably did, were empirical links. It is a matter of empirical investigation to discover whether they existed at all and, if so, to what extent. If it turned out that it was actually *not* the case that the traditional system conduced to stability, moderation and effectiveness, then many readers—and many constitutional commentators—would probably want to view that system in a different light.

There was, however, another kind of argument to be advanced for the traditional British system, one much less dependent on matters of contingent fact. This argument, if anything, was more powerful than any of the others and might well have weighed with large numbers of people even if the other arguments had been found wanting. Moreover, whereas considerations of governmental stability, moderation and effectiveness necessarily arise under any type of political regime—in Iran and Saudi Arabia as well as the United Kingdom—this additional argument, if it has any weight at all, has weight only in a democratic system or at least in a system that is genuinely representative. This is the argument from accountability, which has always been central to the logic of the British system. Under the traditional constitution, British governments, far more than the governments of most other countries, even democratic countries, were straightforwardly and directly accountable to the people whom they claimed to serve. An essential correlate of power hoarding in the UK has always been the government of the day's ultimate accountability to the people for the way in which it has wielded its hoard of power. The people's wisdoms may be vulgar, but in the UK they have always counted for a great deal.

The Americans have a saying: "Throw the rascals out." But, to be able to throw the rascals out, the voters need to know precisely who the rascals are and to have ready to hand an effective mechanism for throwing them out. Moreover, there has to be some real connection, however loose, between the rascals and their responsibilities. There is no point—apart from possibly making one feel good—in throwing out the tribal chief for failing in his duty as rain-maker if someone else is supposed to be responsible for rain-making or if no one is actually capable of making rain. Under those circumstances, assigning responsibility descends easily into mere scapegoating.

The traditional British system met all these requirements almost to perfection. British voters knew who the rascals were: the government of the day. They had ready to hand an effective mechanism for throwing them out: the democratic ballot at a general election. And, thanks to the fact that the British system was largely a power-hoarding system, there was a remarkably close fit between rascals and responsibilities. In the UK, the government of the day was responsible for more or less everything. It could therefore quite reasonably be held to account for more or less everything. A distinguished professor of political science at the University of Chicago expressed the matter thus:

> The line of authority between people and Government [in the United Kingdom] rises singly and directly; the line of responsibility of Cabinet and Parliament to the people descends singly and directly . . . In the British parliamentary system, [the line of authority and responsibility] is undivided and crystal-clear.[14]

Quite so. It was.

Foreigners were often astonished by the neatness and simplicity of it all. Winston Churchill began attending the Potsdam conference in 1945 as Britain's representative. Suddenly, Clement Attlee, with much the same advisors, took his place. James Callaghan was prime minister one day, Margaret Thatcher the next. John Major was prime minister on May 1, 1997. Tony Blair was prime minister on May 2, 1997. The removal van parked overnight in May 1997 in Horse Guards Parade behind 10 Downing Street bore witness to the people's power. General election day was judgment day: singular, unambiguous, decisive, final. Everyone knew what the rules were. Everyone abided by the outcome of the democratic game played according to those rules.

The British took their domestic arrangements more or less for granted, but in fact they were fairly unusual. In the Netherlands, as we saw in the last chapter, government-formation usually owes little, sometimes almost nothing, to what happens on election day. The same goes for many other (though not all) multi-party parliamentary democracies. In the United States, political power is so fragmented—among presidency, Congress and the courts, and between federal, state and local governments—that voters at an election may not have any idea whom to hold to account or how to hold them to account. Divided government in the US—with one party holding the presidency and another frequently holding one or more houses of Congress—further complicates the American electorate's difficulties. One student of American politics has referred, not surprisingly, to a "quite awesome deficit of accountability" inherent in the US system.[15]

The British emphasis on direct, straight and easily understood lines of responsibility and accountability had three virtues. The first was that it empowered the voters. They might not count for much in other ways or on other occasions, but they knew that every four or five years, on general election day, they counted for a very great deal, indeed were decisive. It was this simple fact that made Britain a democracy. It was also this simple fact that almost certainly reconciled the British people to the country's existing political order. Power might be hoarded in the UK, but every few years they, the people, took a share, a big share, of the hoard.

The second virtue of Britain's accountability-centred type of democracy was that it made governments sensitive to public opinion. Those in power might not feel under any moral obligation to listen to the people, let alone to do whatever the people wanted; but, as politicians concerned with their own survival, they knew that on every important issue they had to factor the current state of public opinion on that issue into the relevant political equation. To ignore public opinion, especially towards the end of the life of a Parliament, was an exceedingly risky business. It was a business that those in power seldom got into. Again, the people were thereby empowered—and seemed instinctively to know it. (On the rare occasions when people did not feel empowered in this way and felt they were not being listened to, they could become extremely angry.)

The third virtue of Britain's accountability-centred version of democracy was at least as important as the other two. Precisely because British governments knew that they could be, and would be, held to account, they tended on the whole to behave pretty responsibly. The buck in the UK system stopped with them, they knew it, and most of the time they responded accordingly. British politics was freer than the politics of many other countries from gesture politics, symbolic politics and the disposition to make promises that could not possibly be fulfilled. In power-sharing systems, there is always a temptation for politicians to behave irresponsibly, knowing that nothing dreadful will actually happen as a consequence of what they say or do—someone somewhere else in the system will intervene sooner or later to prevent it—and moreover that, even if something dreadful does happen, blame is most unlikely to attach to them. Complicated and hard-to-understand political systems are, of their nature, accountability-diffusing systems, in which malevolent and dishonest politicians can all too easily take refuge.

This, then, was the traditional UK constitution, with its several traditional virtues: stability, moderation, effectiveness and, above all, strict and proper lines of accountability. That constitution, however, no longer exists. In the next chapter, we consider in some detail how it has changed.

3. THE UNITED KINGDOM CONSTITUTION AMENDED

At the beginning of the new millennium, it takes an effort of will to recall that the British constitution was once widely regarded—not least by the British, but not only by them—as one of the wonders of the political world. As "the Westminster model", it had taken root in most of the countries of the old white Commonwealth. British politicians and civil servants had few qualms about exporting it, or some version of it, to countries as far apart as Asia, sub-Saharan Africa and the Caribbean. Wherever the British flag waved, there could be found a speaker, a mace, a parliament, a prime minister and judges who were often bewigged as well as begowned. British was best. Most everybody knew it.

Here is what an American political scientist had to say about the traditional British system of government in a textbook on comparative politics published in the 1950s:

> Great Britain alone of all the countries dealt with here [France, Germany and the Soviet Union as well as Britain] has managed to maintain, over a long period of time, effective democratic government, if by this we mean a great capacity for constructive action on the part of responsible political leaders. British governments have suffered neither the acute instability nor the near-paralysis that characterized the Weimar Republic and the Third and Fourth Republics in France . . . This inherent capacity for effective action is the truly distinctive characteristic of British government, one it shares with practically no other important democratic system.[1]

And the author did not exclude his own country, the United States, from his analysis.

Nor was admiration for the United Kingdom's constitution confined to the US. A well-known French student of British politics wrote at about the same time:

> The British political system is . . . an enviable model of democratic government. One can only regret that it could not possibly be transplanted to any other country.[2]

In fact, however, efforts *were* made to transplant it to other countries, not only in the British empire but elsewhere. The American Political Science Association in 1950 published a famous report, *Toward a More Responsible Two-party System*, which took Britain's two-party system as its template. Although Douglas MacArthur was himself an American, Japan's postwar Constitution was modelled far more on the British than the American. The writers of the French Constitution of 1958, notably Michel Debré, were great admirers of the British system and, as far as they could, modelled the Fifth Republic's Constitution upon it.

The all but universal admiration for our system of government did not, however, last. Understandably though illogically, Britain's decline in the world seems to have led to a decline in respect for Britain's constitution. With the loss of empire, and America and the Soviet Union's rise to superpower status, Britain's influence in the world rapidly dwindled and outsiders ceased to take any great interest in Britain's internal affairs. The country's relative economic decline and the endemic industrial disruption of the 1960s and 1970s had similar consequences. Why admire the British constitution when there was so little else about Britain deserving of admiration?

In the UK itself, many politicians, journalists and intellectuals came to feel the same way. They railed against the old establishment and the stuffiness, as they saw it, of the Monarchy. They also came to believe there were links between the traditional constitution and both Britain's economic decline and the endemic industrial disruption. A new generation of radical reformers insisted that the country's economic problems were not merely economic in character and that its industrial-relations problems were not merely a matter of tensions on the shop floor. They maintained, instead, that both of these two pathologies were at least partly a consequence of the malfunctioning of Britain's political structures. In particular, they deplored what many of them called "adversarial politics": the politics of contestation and winner take all. Adversarial politics, it was said, led to over-frequent and damaging changes of public policy, with governments of both political parties systematically undoing the work of their predecessors. There was thereby created a climate of profound uncertainty, discouraging to long-term investment and indeed to long-term planning of any kind. Adversarial politics also, it was said, reinforced and helped to perpetuate the "us and them" attitudes so prevalent in industry. Yah-boo politics threatened to create—perhaps had already created—a yah-boo economy and society. As a way out, the reformers of the 1970s looked to electoral reform, the introduction of proportional representation and the formation of continental-style coalition governments. The aim, although it was not put quite like this, was to replace a politics of power hoarding with a politics of power sharing.[3]

The merits of these arguments do not concern us here. What matters for our purposes is that in the late 1960s and 1970s the fundamentals of our traditional constitution began to be called into question for the first time in many generations. The constitution itself was now on the political agenda. It still had its defenders, of course, and the twin forces of habit and inertia were still on its side. But serious questions were now being asked. Doubts had been sown.

The dissatisfaction just described manifested itself at a generalised level: the whole constitution was to be changed. Meanwhile, however, constitutional changes of a more specific character were also being advocated. Some of those pressing for these more limited changes also wanted the whole constitution to be recast, but some did not and most were probably unaware of linkages between the two. Macro changes and micro changes were, to a large extent, advocated separately. At the micro level, one group pressed for home rule for Scotland, another for home rule for Wales. Lawyers and others believed it was time for Britain to have its own bill of rights. Many people on the centre-left of politics, even people who did not envisage a total overhaul of the constitution, nevertheless backed one specific cause: electoral reform. Most members of the Labour Party, for their part, wanted to see the holders of hereditary peerages expelled from the House of Lords. At this issue-by-issue micro level, it was all a bit of a muddle. There was no such thing as an overarching reform "movement".

Nevertheless, by the end of the 20th century, for all manner of reasons, and in all manner of ways, the traditional UK constitution had been transformed. Why it was transformed, and the precise ways in which it came to be transformed, matter less for our purposes than the prodigious scale of the transformation. It is no exaggeration to say that, taken together, the various individual changes amounted to a constitutional revolution. Although few people seem to have noticed the fact, the truth is that the United Kingdom's constitution changed more between 1970 and 2000, and especially between 1997 and 2000, than during any comparable period since at least the middle of the 18th century. As we observed at the end of the last chapter, our traditional constitution no longer exists, although, naturally, important vestiges of it still remain.

II

The vast scale of the transformation is best appreciated if the more important individual changes are enumerated. The list of such changes is a long one. The various items on the list deserve to be ticked off one by one. We begin with a number of items that were not part of any plan or design—indeed in most cases were not recognised as being constitutional changes at all—but which, cumulatively, were of immense significance. These changes crept up on the country unannounced.

First, Europe.

The United Kingdom's entry into the European Economic Community on January 1, 1973 certainly did not have as one of its principal purposes—or indeed as one of its purposes at all—the alteration of the UK's constitution. The motives of successive British governments in promoting British membership of what was then the Common Market were in part economic, in part concerned with finding a new role for Britain in a quite disorienting post-imperial world. Nevertheless, the UK's entry into what is now the European Union had, and is still having, profound constitutional consequences. It is strange that, more than a quarter-century on, so many British politicians still seem so reluctant to accept the reality of these consequences. The Euro-enthusiasts give the impression of wanting to conceal the enormity of what they are doing; the Euro-sceptics give the impression of wanting to conceal the enormity of what has already been done (and can, almost certainly, never be reversed). Agreed on nothing else, the Euro-enthusiasts and Euro-sceptics make a very odd couple.

The original Treaty of Rome changed the United Kingdom's constitution—and the constitutions of all the other EU member states—by creating new supranational institutions with law-making powers. European law constitutes a legal system separate from, and independent of, the legal systems of the member states. More than that, European law does not exist alongside the domestic law of the member states: it takes absolute precedence over it. European law within the member states, including Britain, *is* domestic law. To ensure that this new body of law applies throughout the EU, the Court of Justice of the European Communities exists to enforce it. The Court can fine member states for failing to comply with the law, and the Court's judgments are binding and are not subject to appeal. Only treaty amendments can reverse them.

Developments within the EU since 1973 have further limited the capacity of UK governments—as well as the governments of all the other member states—to act on their own authority. The Single European Act of 1986, the Maastricht Treaty of 1992 and the Amsterdam Treaty of 1997 have all had the effect of extending the remit of the EU's governing bodies and, by extending the principle of qualified majority voting, have also made it much more difficult for individual member states to block proposals for new EU legislation. The arcane arguments over whether or not sovereignty pooled is also sovereignty diminished cannot conceal the fact that the capacity for independent action of all the EU member states, including Britain, has been reduced.

As time has gone on, moreover, the enormous scale of this reduction has at last become apparent. At first, in the 1970s and early 1980s, "Europe" presented itself to the British as a rather remote abstraction; but from the mid 1980s onwards, and with increasing speed, the EU and its institutions have become potent forces in the daily lives of British citizens and—in the present context more important—in the policy making and decision making of British governments. The interpenetration of European and British policy making involves almost every Whitehall department and consumes enormous amounts of ministerial and civil service time, much of it in Brussels and elsewhere on the continent rather than in the UK. The range of subjects dealt with is immense: the Common Agricultural Policy, the Common Fisheries Policy, tobacco advertising, metric weights and measures in shops and supermarkets, the quality of British beaches, regional policy, competition policy, labour law, the free movement of labour, fees in higher education, the axle weights of lorries and a great deal else besides. The British government has a say, and sometimes a veto, in the formulation of European policy in all these areas, but in these and other fields British and European policy are now coterminous. With regard to the EU, the old distinction between "domestic policy" and "foreign policy" no longer applies. Of all the long-term, slow-to-evolve constitutional changes that have taken place over the past three decades, Britain's membership of the EU is undoubtedly the single most important.

It is far, however, from being the only one.

Second, referendums.

No one decided that popular referendums should become part of the British constitution, but they have so become, albeit in a rather hit-and-miss sort of way. The UK's first-ever national referendum was held in June 1975 to confirm (as it turned out) Britain's membership of the European Community; and the debates in Parliament and elsewhere that preceded that referendum did include some discussion of the abstract merits of referendums as a constitutional device. But in the event the Common Market referendum was held, not in response to any considerations of constitutional propriety, but as a straightforward manoeuvre in the internal politics of the Labour Party. One part of the party at that time wanted Britain to pull out of Europe; another part wanted it to stay in. Both sides held their views passionately. Harold Wilson, the party leader—who had previously ruled out holding referendums on Europe or anything else—concluded that promising to hold a referendum on this issue (along with allowing his party's warring factions to fight on opposite sides during the referendum campaign) was the only way of holding the party together. The referendum was duly held, and the outcome was highly satisfactory from Wilson's point of view. Britain stayed in. The Labour Party, for the time being, did not fall apart.

Wilson's manoeuvre, however politically ingenious, was dismissed at the time as cynical—it was certainly not justified on any higher plane—and, perhaps partly for that reason, two further decades passed before any new national referendums were seriously proposed. When they were, the issues were, again, constitutional, and, again, the political parties that initially proposed them were internally divided. Promising a national referendum became a handy device for (a) postponing an issue ("kicking it into the long grass"), (b) preventing it from causing too much mayhem within the party promoting the referendum and (c) cloaking that party—or at least trying to cloak it—in the garb of democratic respectability. John Smith in 1993 promised that, if and when the Labour Party returned to power, it would hold a referendum on reform of the electoral system, a promise confirmed by Tony Blair in 1996 and in Labour's 1997 election manifesto. John Major in 1996 promised that, if at any stage his government proposed to take Britain into the single Europe currency (the euro), a referendum on the issue would be held. Blair had given the same undertaking on Labour's behalf by the end of the same year.

These were to be national referendums. Neither referendum, at the time of writing, has been held. But Tony Blair, during his three years as opposition leader between 1994 and 1997, also promised the Scots their referendum on devolution, the Welsh their referendum also on devolution and Londoners their referendum on the creation of a new Greater London authority. By the time he came to power in 1997, Blair had thus categorically promised four referendums and more conditionally promised a fifth (if his government decided to take Britain into the euro). He later pledged himself to a sixth referendum: on the 1998 Good

Friday agreement affecting Northern Ireland. Four of the referendums—the ones in Scotland, Wales, London and Northern Ireland—were held within roughly two years of Labour's coming to power. All four turned out more or less satisfactorily from the government's point of view. The other two, at the time of writing, pend.

The referendum has not yet become firmly established as a part of the UK constitution. There is no national statute governing the conduct of referendums (though there is one governing their financing); and there is certainly no broad agreement on when, and on what subjects, referendums should be held. It is still possible to imagine a confident and united government with a large parliamentary majority pushing through major constitutional changes without the benefit of popular referendums; the 1986 Single European Act and the 1998-99 removal of most of the hereditary peers from the House of Lords are arguably two such instances. Nevertheless, referendums are now legitimate, allowable and frequently called for in a way that was inconceivable in the past. Opposition parties in future will increasingly demand referendums on major issues, and governments will increasingly find those demands hard to resist—and, of course, are likely to have their own reasons for finding the referendum device useful. The idea of holding referendums, if not yet the habit of holding them, has entered the nation's (and the nations') political bloodstream. It will not soon be eradicated.

Third, the changing position of local government.

We noted in the last chapter that local government in the UK, especially in the three decades after 1945, enjoyed a substantial measure of local autonomy and also provided a wide range of public services. Local government was at once free and strong—a veritable estate of the realm, far more so than the civil service.

Beginning in the late 1960s, however, and accelerating after 1979, the hitherto secure position of local government within the constitution was subject to sustained attack. In the famous phrase of a Labour environment minister, Anthony Crosland, "The party's over." He was referring specifically to high levels of local government spending, but his phrase was seen in time to have a far wider resonance. Successive governments, but especially the Thatcher and Major governments of the 1980s and 1990s, had a wide variety of reasons for wishing to bring local government under tighter central control and also for wishing (in the jargon of the time) to downsize it. They did not want their macroeconomic policies undermined by the taxing and spending policies of local governments. They sought to maintain or establish truly national standards of service provision. They believed, not without reason, that some local authorities were inefficient, incompetent and even corrupt. The Thatcher Government, in particular, took exception to the fact that in the 1980s many of the largest local authorities were in the hands of what she regarded as "loony left" Labour councils. In governments of both parties, ministers behaved in ways that indicated that they really rather fancied central control for its own sake.

Whatever central governments' motives, the effects were felt by local authorities throughout the country. By the end of the 20th century, UK local authorities' room for policy manoeuvre, never enormous, had been drastically reduced. In the field of education, where they had once enjoyed so much freedom, they and the schools under their (increasingly nominal) control were subject for the first time to a centrally imposed national curriculum supplemented by centrally imposed tests of pupil attainment. Both Conservative and Labour governments also sought to impose on local authorities their views about whether secondary schools should be organised along comprehensive or selective lines. The ways in which local schools were managed increasingly came under central government supervision and control. On the financial side, the spending plans of individual local authorities—not just of the local authority sector as a whole—were more and more dictated by central government, as was the ability of local authorities to determine how much revenue they wished to raise locally. At one stage, so-called "rate-capping", followed by "charge-capping", was imposed. By the end of the 20th century, a mere 20 per cent (or thereabouts) of total local government revenues in the UK were being generated from genuinely local sources.

Local government was thus being imprisoned. At the same time, it was being disembowelled. In the two decades after the war, local authorities in Britain did more and more; in the three decades or so since then, they have done less and less. They have increasingly become (again in the jargon of the time) service enablers rather than service providers. Refuse collection, leisure facilities, residential homes for the elderly, buses and trams, municipal car parks, professional services like architecture and computer-software design—all these and many more have been subjected to compulsory competitive tendering, with substantial transfers of capital assets from the local authority to the private sector and with more and more local services provided by private or quasi-private organisations.

In no field has the shrinking of the scale of local authority activity been greater than in the field of housing. British local authorities were once among the greatest house-builders and landlords of Europe. In 1950, for example, local councils built 169,221 houses; in 1960 they built 127,412; in 1970 they built 171,595. But by 1980 their total was down to 86,027, and by 1990 it was down to 16,563—scarcely 10 per cent of the total forty years before. By 2000 local-authority house building had virtually ground to a halt.[4] The slow-down and then the virtual cessation of council house building, together with the sale of council houses and flats to their tenants, meant that the number of people living in council-owned dwellings also fell sharply. Total local government spending, having risen steadily throughout the 1950s and 1960s, thereafter levelled off.

Thus, by the end of the last century, local government had become, as it has remained since, a mere shadow of its former self—a long shadow, to be sure, but one lacking the sheer physical substance it once possessed. Local government has surrendered, has been forced to surrender, the larger part of its traditional autonomy. It has ceased to be an estate of the realm. Ironically, just as in the case of the constitutional changes wrought by Britain's membership of the EU, there has been a certain reluctance to acknowledge publicly how much the constitutional position of British local government has changed. Central government ministers, of both parties, are reluctant to confess to the full enormity of what they have done; a large proportion of those in local government are reluctant to admit to the full enormity of what has been done to them. The former do not wish to appear dictatorial; the latter do not wish to appear feeble. Once again, they make a strange pair of co-conspirators.

Fourth, the increase in judicial review—another case of creeping, as distinct from consciously willed, constitutional change.

For most of its long history, certainly for most of the 20th century, the British judiciary in no way saw itself as an active player in the British political system. It did not see itself as a potential adversary either of government in general or of the government of the day in particular. On the contrary, British judges not only could not, under our constitution, challenge Acts of Parliament: they were also reluctant to challenge decisions of the executive. The Queen's judges, although independent of the Queen's ministers, showed themselves exceedingly reluctant to gainsay them. The judges almost always behaved as though, tacitly, they and the Queen's ministers were on the same side. Hence the point made in the last chapter about the British judiciary not being, or acting as, an autonomous centre of power within the system.

However, even before the coming into force of the Human Rights Act (of which more later), the judges were beginning to stir.

Judges in this country have always had the power in law to strike down the acts of government ministers, their officials and other government agencies on the ground that they have acted *ultra vires*—have exceeded the powers expressly given them by statute—or have acted contrary to the principles of natural justice. Moreover, whereas before the 1960s the judges had almost never made use of that power, starting in that decade they began to do so: not often, but with much greater frequency than in the past. The change appears to have come about because senior judges believed that the state—in the hands of governments of both political parties—was too often acting arbitrarily and too often encroaching on the liberties of the subject.

An early landmark decision was that of the House of Lords in the case of *Conway v. Rimmer* in 1968, when the court rejected the then Labour Home Secretary's contention that the disclosure of government documents relevant to the case would be contrary to the public interest. A quarter-century later, in 1993, another Home Secretary, this time a Conservative, found himself adjudged in contempt of court for failing to abide by the order of a lower court in an asylum case. A subsequent Conservative Home Secretary, Michael Howard, seemed almost to court, even to relish, judicial disapproval of his ministerial actions; he certainly came in for a great deal of it. Throughout, the judges have been cautious in pushing out the boundaries of their traditional role; but push them out they have, displaying an increasing willingness to question not only ministers' procedures but their reasoning. Along the way, the judges have made major incursions into the old, once nearly sacrosanct doctrine of Crown (that is, executive) immunity.

Moreover, as so often happens, supply has created its own demand. Sensing that the judiciary was in the process of expanding its role, individuals, business firms and other organisations have become increasingly given to initiating judicial review proceedings. The number of applications for judicial review rose from roughly 500 a year in the early 1980s, to roughly 2,000 a year in the early 1990s, to well over 4,000 a year by the early 2000s.[5] Lord Rees-Mogg, an elderly journalist, even sought judicial review—unsuccessfully, as it turned out—to challenge the 1992 Treaty of Maastricht. To be sure, high-profile cases such as Lord Rees-Mogg's remain a rarity. A large proportion of all applications for judicial review are lodged against local authorities, health authorities and other quangos rather than against ministers; and most applications—probably as many as three-quarters—fail. But that is not the point. In the first place, a few cases succeed, and the courts' decisions in at least some of those cases have had the effect of significantly changing the law. In the second place, the fact that the law has been changed and that judicial review is now an option available to aggrieved citizens means that the possibility of judicial intervention has to be factored into an ever-increasing range of ministerial and other governmental and quasi-governmental decisions. The judges, even before the Human Rights Act, had already re-emerged on the political scene.

Fifth, the party system.

Changes in a country's party system, however radical, are not normally considered to be changes in that country's constitution. Even in terms of the definition of "constitution" offered on the first page of this book—"a set of the most important rules . . ."—it may be stretching things a bit to refer to recent changes in Britain's party system as being constitutional changes. That said, the way in which a country's party system operates affects the functioning of every other aspect of that country's politics. A country's party system, if not quite a rule of the game, is a factor profoundly conditioning the way in which the game is played. To take an obvious example, the political system of the Fifth Republic in France, as compared with that of the Fourth, was transformed not only by the adoption in 1958 of a new capital-C Constitution but, if anything, even more by the consolidation of the French party system into two relatively stable competing party blocs, left-wing and right-wing (the Socialists and their allies and the Gaullists and theirs). In France, party change led to system change.

In Britain, without anyone in particular having willed it, the party system over the past three decades has been radically altered—along two separate dimensions.

In the first place, British voters' willingness to vote for political parties other than the two main parties has increased strikingly, almost dramatically, since the early 1970s. We saw in the last chapter that at all ten general elections held between 1931 and 1970 the Conservative and Labour parties always won more than 85 per cent of the popular vote and frequently won more than 90 per cent. Nothing like that has happened since. At the seven general elections held between February 1974 and May 1997, the two main parties never won as much as 85 per cent of the vote, and on five of the seven occasions their combined share of the vote fell to 75 per cent or less.[6] In other words, at each of the seven general elections over the past quarter-century roughly a quarter of those who have bothered to turn out have deliberately wasted their vote in the sense that they voted for a party that they knew had no realistic chance of forming the next government. They have deliberately chosen *not* to regard the electoral choice facing them as a dichotomous choice. It would appear that in many cases, though not all, voters have been equally repelled by both of the main parties.

In the second place, the party system has ceased to be truly national. The Conservative and Labour parties continue to be the main contenders at Westminster elections in England, but in Scotland and Wales, although Labour remains one of the two main parties, the Conservatives are no longer Labour's sole or even principal electoral rivals. In Scotland, the Conservatives have not won as much as 30 per cent of the vote since 1979, and in 1997 they actually dropped into third place behind the Scottish National Party. Following the 1997 election, the Tories, who had held 23 Scottish seats in 1970, held none. In Wales, the Conservatives have contrived to remain in second place in terms of their share of the vote, but the Welsh Tories have not won as much as 30 per cent of the vote since 1983, and following the 1997 election they, too, like their Scottish counterparts, held no Westminster seats at all.[7] In that electoral sense, Great Britain has ceased to be one nation.

What these changes in the party system mean for the functioning of the British constitution will be considered in the next chapter.

III

As has been repeatedly emphasised, the changes to the constitution considered in the previous section—those resulting from the UK's membership of the European Union, the coming of referendums, the decline in local government's autonomy, the rise of judicial review and the increasing fragmentation of the British party system—were in most cases not willed by anyone. They were certainly not willed as part of some grand constitutional design. They just happened. In 1997, however, a new Labour government came to power which *was* committed to an extensive programme of constitutional change and which, in the years since, has largely, if not wholly, implemented that programme. Since 1997 the unplanned and accidental has given way to the self-conscious and deliberate. The post-1997 constitutional changes also require to be enumerated. It seems sensible to continue with the same sequence of numbers.

Sixth, the handing over of control over interest rates to the Bank of England.

Control over interest rates in the UK had been the prerogative of the Chancellor of the Exchequer since the nationalisation of the Bank of England in 1946; but on May 6, 1997, within four days of taking office, Gordon Brown, the new Labour Chancellor of the Exchequer, startled both the political and the financial communities by announcing that henceforth interest rates would be set not by him but by the Bank of England in the form of a new nine-member Monetary Policy Committee. At a stroke, Brown in 1997 surrendered not merely the Chancellor of the Exchequer's control, but the whole government's control, over a key element—probably *the* key element—in the determination of monetary policy.

It may strike the reader as odd that this particular development should be listed under the heading of constitutional changes; but it *was* a constitutional change. It altered completely one of the most important rules governing the relations among the organs of the government in the UK; it simultaneously created, in the form of the Bank's Monetary Policy Committee, a new source of autonomous power in the British system. The analogous American experience is relevant here. America's capital-C Constitution makes no mention of the Federal Reserve Board, which was not created until 1913 and, even then, by means of a federal statute rather than a formal constitutional amendment; but almost all observers of American government today would accept that the Federal Reserve, in particular its chairman, is now an integral part of America's small-c constitution. At any time in the 1990s, any account of the workings of the US government that failed to give a prominent place to Alan Greenspan would have been seriously deficient.

Seventh, devolution to Scotland and Wales—universally acknowledged to be a constitutional change of the utmost importance.

Unlike the handing over of interest rate policy to the Bank of England, the twin causes of home rule for Scotland and Wales had been the subject of on-and-off political debate for more than a hundred years. At the time of the controversies over home rule for Ireland, there had also been talk of "home rule all round" for the UK; and a string of SNP electoral successes in the late 1960s and mid 1970s provoked the Labour governments of that era into proposing quite radical devolution measures for both Scotland and Wales. To an extent now largely forgotten, the parliamentary timetable of the late 1970s was dominated first by a combined Scotland and Wales Bill and then by separate bills for each of the two nations. The Scotland and Wales Bill failed to reach the statute book. The separate bills did;

but a negative referendum in Wales killed the Welsh bill, and a similar referendum in Scotland failed to secure the required majority for the Scottish legislation. Plaid Cymru and the SNP thereupon withdrew their support from the government of James Callaghan, precipitating its fall in March 1979.

As a live political issue, devolution then went into hibernation for more than a decade. As a political cause, however, it quietly and unobtrusively gained in strength, especially north of the border. Large numbers of Scots came to dislike intensely being governed from London. At general elections, the majority of Scots voted Labour, Liberal Democrat or SNP; the majority of English (or at least a substantial plurality of them) voted Conservative. As the English vastly outnumbered the Scots, it was English preferences that prevailed. UK government from 1979 onwards was English—and therefore, to the Scots, alien—government. Largely unnoticed south of the border, a do-it-yourself, non-statutory Scottish Constitutional Convention, supported by Labour, the Liberal Democrats, the Scottish Trades Union Congress and most of the Scottish churches, met from 1989 onwards to draw up an ambitious plan for Scottish self-government short of outright independence. The Labour Party took up the Scottish scheme, developed its own more modest proposals for Wales and undertook in its 1997 election manifesto to introduce at an early date devolution measures for both countries. The subsequent referendums in Scotland and Wales carried (though the one in Wales only narrowly), and the new government's devolution legislation took effect in 1999.

The devolution of central government power to Scotland was on a prodigious scale. There has probably never in any country been a greater voluntary handover of power by any national government to any subnational government. In typically British fashion, the handover was widely dismissed as a detail, a modest evolutionary step, a minor constitutional adjustment. Or, rather, it was widely so dismissed south of the border. The Scots knew better. Scotland, with a population of 5.1 million—larger than the populations of Finland and Norway and almost as large as that of Denmark—in 1999 became effectively a state within the state.

Under the terms of the Scotland Act 1998, the London-based central government retains control over macroeconomic policy and the social security system. It also retains control over foreign and defence policy and over the Scotland-wide electoral system (though not over the electoral systems for Scottish local authorities). But everything else, virtually the whole of domestic policy and administration, is handed over to the new Scottish

Parliament and Executive: economic development, local government, the environment, agriculture and fisheries (subject, of course, to EU constraints), personal social services, education, including university education, law and order, public health and health services, transport, housing—the lot. In area after area, Whitehall's writ no longer runs north of the border. Even Scots sometimes say, for example, that they are now in charge of running the National Health Service north of the border. That is true but is only part of the truth: the Scottish Parliament could, if it chose to, *abolish* the National Health Service north of the border, so great is its power.

At the heart of the new arrangements for Scotland, there lies, however, an anomaly. The Scots largely control their own expenditure. They do not, however, control their own revenue. The Scottish Parliament can, as is well known, vary the rate of income tax levied north of the border by 3 pence in either direction; but otherwise Scotland remains, even more than English local authorities, fiscally dependent on the United Kingdom Treasury. Under the terms of the Scotland Act, the great bulk of the Scottish Parliament and Executive's revenue derives from a single, enormous block grant from the centre. Whether this somewhat lopsided arrangement can persist indefinitely we shall consider in the next chapter.

The extent of the devolution of power to Wales is, of course, substantially more limited. All primary legislation for Wales is still Westminster legislation, and the new Welsh Assembly is restricted to determining the content of secondary legislation under existing Westminster laws. Unlike the Scottish Parliament, the Welsh Assembly has neither tax-raising nor tax-varying powers and is utterly dependent on London for the whole of its revenue. One hope for the Welsh Assembly is that it will enable the Principality's elected politicians to regain control of governmental functions that before the Wales Act had fallen increasingly into the hands of unelected quangos; but, although such a development, if it occurred on a large scale, would affect the balance of power within Wales, it would have only a negligible effect on the balance of power between Cardiff and the government in London.

Eighth, devolution to Northern Ireland.

In the 25 years between the reimposition of direct rule in 1972 and the Labour Party's return to power in 1997, successive governments attempted to work out some sort of compromise arrangement that would bring an end to violence in the Province and enable the Protestant/Unionist majority and the Catholic/Republican minority to work together politically. All the attempts failed. The Sunningdale Agreement of 1973 led to the setting up of a power-sharing executive for the Province; but that experiment in Unionist-Republican co-operation was short-lived, destroyed in 1974 by the Ulster Workers' Council strike. The Thatcher Government in the early 1980s tentatively launched a programme of "rolling devolution", but that, too, sank without trace, and the 1985 Anglo-Irish Agreement did more to improve relations between London and Dublin than it did, at least in the short term, to improve relations between the hostile camps in the North. The same was true of both the 1993 Downing Street Declaration between the United Kingdom and Ireland and the two countries' Joint Framework Document of 1995. The most that had been achieved by 1997—but it was a lot—was the establishment of a degree of mutual trust between some of Northern Ireland's leading politicians, both Unionist and Republican.

Tony Blair came to power determined to bring peace to Northern Ireland if he could, and he devoted a great deal of his time and energy during his first year in office—probably more than most people realise—to brokering a deal in the Province. The outcome was the Good Friday Agreement of 1998. The Agreement's provisions were complex, involving, among other things, intergovernmental co-operation between London and Dublin, cross-border co-operation between the Republic and the North, the policing of Northern Ireland, the decommissioning of weapons and the early release of prisoners. But there were, and are, two features of the Agreement with UK-wide constitutional implications.

The first, as in the cases of Scotland and Wales, concerns the scale of the devolution of power under the Agreement from London to Belfast. In this respect, the Northern Ireland arrangements resemble the Scottish far more than they do the Welsh. The new Northern Ireland Assembly is intended to fall heir to almost all the powers, both executive and legislative, exercised since the reimposition of direct rule by the Secretary of State for Northern Ireland. These range widely, as in Scotland, over the fields of economic development, employment, health, education, agriculture and the environment. The most important field of activity delegated to the Scottish Parliament but not to be delegated, at least at the outset, to the Northern Ireland Assembly is—hardly surprisingly given the peculiar circumstances of Northern Ireland—law and order. Policing and the criminal justice system for the time being remain the responsibility of the London-based Secretary of State.

The second feature is the more interesting and is, given the constitutional history of the UK as a whole, by a wide margin the more remarkable. The peculiar circumstances of Northern Ireland set the negotiators of the Good Friday Agreement two problems. The first was that Northern Ireland was deeply divided into two communities: the Protestant/Unionist and the Catholic/Republican. These two communities by and large lived apart, worked apart, ate apart, drank apart and, if they worshipped at all, worshipped apart. If they did not actively hate each other, they certainly feared each other. The other problem was that one of these two communities, the Protestant/Unionist, was considerably larger than the other. In any referendum or Westminster-style election that pitted the Protestant/Unionists against the Catholic/Republicans, the Protestant/Unionists would always win. They always did. The main function of elections in Northern Ireland was merely to provide the Protestant/Unionists with periodic opportunities to reassert their majority status. Those who negotiated the Good Friday Agreement had therefore to find some means of both (i) bringing together the two divided communities in a new set of political structures and (ii) ensuring that the Protestant/Unionist majority could never take advantage of these new structures to impose its will on the minority Catholic/Republican community.

Against this background, it is perhaps not surprising that the new political structures devised in the course of the Good Friday negotiations are almost a parody—using the word in a wholly benign sense—of the political structures of the Netherlands. The English find the Northern Ireland Assembly and its workings weird, complicated and alien. The Dutch, if they were there, would feel right at home. They would be dismayed by the depths of the divisions between the two communities, and they would regret that one of the two communities enjoys a permanent majority status (the Dutch are accustomed to everyone being in a minority); but they would instantly recognise the political logic inherent in the Good Friday Agreement's terms. As in the Netherlands, the guiding principles of the new political arrangements for Northern Ireland are intended to be inclusivity, power-sharing and proportionality.

The new Northern Ireland Assembly is large (108 members) in order to ensure that almost every political grouping in the Province can be accommodated. Its members are elected, as in the Netherlands, by a system of proportional representation. Ministerial portfolios, the chairmanships of Assembly committees and the memberships of those committees are allocated in proportion to the parties' numerical strength in the Assembly. The First Minister presides over a multi-party cabinet which he is in no conceivable position to dominate (except perhaps, rarely, by sheer force of personality). Moreover, the Northern Ireland cabinet is, like most Dutch cabinets, "over-sized" in the sense of comprising representatives of more parties than are required to secure an absolute majority in the Assembly.

But, of course, the Northern Ireland arrangements have to go further than those in the Netherlands. They have to deal with the elemental fact that one community and its elected representatives are permanently in the majority; they have to ensure that the minority is in a position effectively to protect its interests. The procedures devised for achieving this purpose under the Good Friday Agreement include both "parallel consent", with majorities of both the Unionist and Nationalist delegations in the Assembly having to approve of designated measures, and "weighted majorities", with 60 per cent of members having to vote in favour, the 60 per cent to include at least 40 per cent of each of the two delegations. The terms of the Agreement also ensure that, in practice, the Deputy First Minister will be from the minority community and that the cabinet will not merely be over-sized but will include Catholic/Republican as well as Protestant/Unionist ministers. In the Good Friday Agreement's own words, the aim has been to put in place "safeguards to ensure that all sections of the community can participate and work together successfully in the operation of these institutions and that all sections of the community are protected".[8] The aim, in other words, has been to put in place Northern Ireland's own version of the Netherlands' consociational democracy.

Whether the aims of those who negotiated the Good Friday Agreement will be achieved is still, in the early spring of 2001, unclear. Everything depends on the willingness of the leaders of the two communities to make the new system work, and both sets of leaders are under continuous pressure from their followers not to make unwarranted concessions to the other side. The Dutch long ago decided to live together politically, almost come what may; the two communities in Northern Ireland have made no such decision. The Dutch enthusiasm for compromise is matched in Northern Ireland by an almost equal suspicion of compromise. It is now, and will be in the future, much harder to reach consensus in Northern Ireland than in the Netherlands. That said, if the terms of the Good Friday Agreement do prove workable in the long term, an entirely new set of political ideas and institutions will have been injected into, or at least added onto, the United Kingdom's traditional constitution.

Ninth, the creation of a new local authority for London.

Ever since the Thatcher Government's abolition of the obstreperous (according to Thatcher) Greater London Council in 1985, the Labour Party had been pledged to the recreation of some kind of democratically elected London-wide body. By the time the Blair Government came to power in 1997, however, it was clear that it would be inordinately expensive, and probably also widely unpopular, to effect a massive transfer of powers from the 32 London boroughs to the new London body, and it was therefore decided that the new body should be assigned a mainly coordinating and promotional role rather than an executive one. The powers and resources of the new body were to be tightly circumscribed. The Labour government also feared that, if the new authority were given extensive powers and if it then fell into the wrong hands politically, it could turn out to prove, at best, a considerable embarrassment to the central government and, at worst, an effective challenger for its authority. The new London body would, after all, have a legitimate claim to represent 7.3 million people—more than the populations of Scotland and Northern Ireland put together. In addition, the contumacious Ken Livingstone, who had given both Margaret Thatcher and Neil Kinnock's Labour Party such a hard time in the 1980s, was still on the political scene and still cast a long shadow ahead of him.

In the event, the Greater London Authority Act 1999 gives the new Greater London Authority, and especially its directly elected Mayor, a good deal of potential political leverage but very little in the way of actual political power. It remains to be seen whether, and under what circumstances, the leverage can be turned into power. The new Authority's central task is to devise, in consultation with the 32 boroughs and other interested parties, strategic plans for dealing with such London-wide issues as transport, economic development, air quality, waste disposal and culture and the arts. Specialist bodies, with substantial inputs from the Greater London Authority and its Mayor, have also been created, covering transport, economic development, land-use planning, fire and emergency services and, not least, the Metropolitan Police. For the first time since 1829, political control of London's police force has passed from the Home Secretary in Whitehall to a local police authority. Because the new Greater London Authority has so few executive powers, its total budget is not expected to exceed roughly £30 million annually, most of it derived, as in the case of Scotland, from central government grants.

Whatever the new London Authority's precise powers (or, rather, lack of them), there is every reason to believe that

London's elected Mayor, like Scotland's First Minister and Wales's First Secretary, will rapidly become the personal embodiment of local aspirations and grievances and an effective advocate—or at least a loud advocate—of local causes. Local and national voices are now being heard in the British system in a way they have not been heard for more than a hundred years.

Tenth, new electoral systems.

Except in Northern Ireland, voters throughout the United Kingdom until very recently cast their ballots in the straightforward manner dictated by the first-past-the-post electoral system. The voter put a cross next to the name of one and only one candidate. The candidate with the most votes won, even if his or her total fell far short of an absolute majority. The system was used in Westminster elections, in elections to the European Parliament and, with minor variations (to allow for multi-member wards), in local government elections. The first-past-the-post system was the only system that British voters knew. A different system, the single transferable vote, was used in Northern Ireland, and only in Northern Ireland, for all elections except those to the UK Parliament at Westminster.

In the past few years, however, simplicity has given way to complexity, stale uniformity to almost infinite variety. Elections to the Westminster Parliament and local elections in England, Wales and (for the time being) Scotland are still conducted under first-past-the-post, but elections to the European Parliament are conducted on the basis of a regional-list system similar to those widely used on the European continent while elections to the Scottish Parliament and the Welsh Assembly employ an additional-member system similar to that used in Germany. London mayoral elections employ a device called the supplementary vote while London Assembly elections, like those for the Scottish Parliament and the Welsh Assembly, use a version of the additional-member system. Londoners with a taste for voting under different systems are especially favoured. They are able to cast their ballots under no fewer than four systems: first-past-the-post (Westminster Parliament and London boroughs), regional list (European Parliament), additional-member (London Assembly) and supplementary vote (London Mayor). The citizens of few other democratic countries have such a cornucopia of riches available to them.

The proliferation of electoral systems not only constitutes a major constitutional change in itself: it has had, at least in some parts of the UK, major constitutional consequences. The abandonment of first-past-the-post in Scotland virtually guarantees (as those attending the Scottish Constitutional Convention meant that it should) that no single party will ever have an overall majority in the Scottish Parliament and that minority or coalition governments will be the norm. For at least the duration of the first Parliament, the Labour Party and the Liberal Democrats have chosen coalition. The abandonment of first-past-the-post in Wales also makes it highly likely, though by no means certain, that no single party will have an overall majority in the Welsh Assembly. The Labour Party in Wales duly failed to win 50 per cent of the seats in the Assembly at the first election, and a brief period of Labour minority administration was followed in due course by the formation of another Labour-Liberal Democrat coalition. In London, the newly elected Mayor, the aforementioned Ken Livingstone, chose for reasons of his own to form a broadly based administration, comprising members of all parties and none. By the winter of 2000–2001, single-party government in the UK was confined to Westminster/Whitehall and a number—admittedly a large number—of local authorities.

Eleventh, the Human Rights Act, which came into force in Scotland in July 1999, in Northern Ireland in December 1999 and in England and Wales in October 2000.

The United Kingdom became a signatory of the European Convention on Human Rights shortly after the Second World War and in the mid 1960s went further, granting its citizens full legal access to the European Court of Human Rights in Strasbourg. In doing so, the UK committed itself—in fact, if not in legal form—to acquiescing in the judgments of the European Court of Human Rights and, if necessary, to amending UK law to bring it into conformity with the Court's rulings. Over the years, the UK government was from time to time taken to the Court, and the Court from time to time found in favour of the complainants and against UK ministers and UK law. In a well-publicised case in 1998, for example, *Bowman v. United Kingdom*, the Court ruled that British law was at fault in preventing someone from spending a small amount of her own money opposing the election of a particular parliamentary candidate when UK law placed no national or regional restrictions on spending by political parties.

Despite UK citizens' occasional successes in going to the Strasbourg Court, it soon, however, became widely accepted that the existing arrangements were unsatisfactory. As a matter of principle, it seemed strange that UK citizens could obtain legal redress for human rights violations by their own government only in a foreign, or foreign-seeming, court. In practice, cases taken to the Strasbourg Court were costly to pursue and subject to interminable delays. As early as 1974, Lord Scarman, in his Hamlyn Lectures of that year, called for a British bill of rights, and by the mid 1980s the view was widely held on the left and centre-left of politics, and also among the legal profession, that there should be such a bill of rights and also that it should take the form of straightforwardly incorporating the European Convention on Human Rights into British domestic law. The Labour Party promised a measure along these lines in its 1997 election manifesto.

The Human Rights Act 1998 does incorporate the European Convention, with minor modifications, into UK domestic law. From now on, ministers, at the time of introducing new legislation, are required to certify that the proposed legislation is compatible with the terms of the Convention. Judges in Britain are similarly required to give effect to the Convention's provisions "so far as it is possible to do so". If courts decide that acts by the government, local authorities or other public bodies are in violation of the Convention, they can strike them down. They can also strike down pieces of secondary legislation that are held to be in violation. The courts are not empowered to strike down primary legislation (that is, Acts of Parliament) in the manner of constitutional courts in some other countries, but the higher courts, at least, *are* empowered to declare that a specific piece of primary legislation does, in their judgment, violate the Convention's terms. If a higher court does so decide on any occasion, government ministers can take advantage of a new fast-track procedure to amend the legislation that has caused offence. These latter provisions are designed to ensure that Parliament, rather than the judiciary, remains legally sovereign. Whether there are circumstances in which a government minister would choose not to take advantage of the new fast-track procedure remains to be seen.

No one can know until the Human Rights Act has been in force for a considerable period of time how great its cumulative impact will be. Most of the Act's supporters take the view that the volume of litigation will not increase substantially under the Act and that, even if it does, the judges, exercising their usual restraint, will be reluctant to challenge the authority of Parliament and the executive without having substantial grounds for so doing. On the other hand, there are many, mostly among the Act's opponents, who fear that there could be an explosion of litigation under the terms of the Act and that, given half a chance, the courts could run amok, as, in their view, they have in the United States. Only time will tell. But what is clear is that the potential role of the judiciary in the UK—and probably its actual role—will increase substantially as a result of the Act. The courts are bound to strike down acts of the executive from time to time, they are bound to call specific pieces of legislation into question, and, as in the case of the extension of judicial review, government ministers and everyone else in public authorities, when they make decisions, are bound to have in mind the courts' probable or possible future behaviour. How great the change to our constitution will prove to be must remain in doubt, but that there will be a substantial change is beyond question.

Twelfth, the House of Lords.

The House of Lords, as we noted in the last chapter, has not been a significant player in our constitutional system since the passage of the Parliament Act 1911—and it became even more insignificant following the passage of the Parliament Act 1949. Since the late 1940s, the House of Lords has frequently been useful, has occasionally been influential and has from time to time been a nuisance (especially to Labour ministers); but it has not for any sustained period constituted an autonomous source of power within the system.

It has nevertheless remained in existence and remained controversial. Most members of the Labour and Liberal Democrat parties have objected to the fact that a majority of the House's members have been hereditary peers and, as such, symbols of class privilege. Most members of the same two parties have resented even more the fact that, as a result of the hereditary peers' presence in the Lords, the Conservative Party, whether in or out of office, has enjoyed a permanent majority in the Upper House. From another angle, many constitutional reformers have argued, not merely that the personal and partisan composition of the House of Lords should be reformed, but that the House—possibly directly elected, possibly with a new name—should be given augmented powers to amend legislation, to scrutinise the executive and to act as protector of civil liberties and the constitution. In other words, reformist ideas about the future of the House of Lords have ranged all the way from advocating outright abolition to favouring a new Second Chamber with elected members and powers not dissimilar to those of the United States Senate.

The government elected in 1997 came to power committed to no more, but no less, than removing completely the hereditary peers from the House of Lords and ensuring that in future no one political party, whether the Conservatives or anyone else, could ever have an absolute majority in the House. That was to be stage one of reform. Stage two was to consist of a more radical overhaul of the Upper House, along lines as yet unspecified. The government acted swiftly on stage one, and the House of Lords Act 1999 removed all but 92 of the "hereditaries" (as they had become known) from the House; the 92 were to be allowed to remain for only a limited period. As regards stage two of reform, the government, unsure of what it wanted to do or what was politically feasible, in 1999 appointed an all-party and no-party Royal Commission on the Reform of the House of Lords to enquire into the whole matter. When the Commission reported at the end of 1999, it recommended a new Second Chamber with an elected element and with, the Commission hoped, increased authority and political credibility. At the time of writing, the government seemed inclined to accept the broad recommendations of the Royal Commission's report but had not yet done so.

Whatever the final shape of the new House of Lords (or Senate or Second Chamber or Upper House or whatever it is ultimately called), two things seem certain. One is that the new body will not be given either powers or authority sufficient to enable it to challenge the democratically elected House of Commons; the new body, in other words, will not become a US Senate or anything like it. The other, however, is that, because the hereditary peers will have been removed, and because the new body will have been founded on a more rational and democratic basis than the old one, the new Upper House is bound to be a more assertive and therefore more influential body than its predecessor. There were already signs in 1999–2000 of a new assertiveness—even a new aggressiveness—in the existing House of Lords, once most of the hereditary peers had been removed. The fully reformed body will certainly want to continue on that basis. By, say, the year 2010, the new Upper House will by no means have recovered the enormous power forfeited by the House of Lords in 1911, but it will be substantially more significant in political terms than the old House had become by 1997.

Thus, twelve constitutional changes, most of them major, in the space of only three decades: a kind of Glorious Revolution of the late 20th century. Whether the changes are truly glorious is open to dispute. Revolutionary they undoubtedly are.

Moreover, accompanying this round-dozen of constitutional changes has been another change, not exactly in the constitution itself, but in the political atmosphere in which the constitution has its being. This additional change is important and is worth noting.

In the last chapter, we emphasised the traditional constitution's insistence on a quite strict division of labour between governors and governed. The government was to govern. The governed were to be governed, except that every four or five years they were to be allowed to choose their governors. Even after the coming of democracy early in the last century, the relationship between governors and governed in the UK retained a certain hierarchical quality. Radio and television interviewers were polite to the point of being deferential. There was a tendency—not to be overstated, but real—for British citizens to look up to and trust those placed in authority over them. It was not thought utterly absurd when someone said shortly after the war, "The man in Whitehall knows best."

That was then. In the present context, it hardly needs to be pointed out that now is now and that over the past few decades British political discourse has become altogether more egalitarian, sceptical and oppositional in style. The man who once knew best is now widely dismissed as knowing nothing—and quite possibly as being self-serving and wicked into the bargain. The "romantic revolution" of the 1960s took a heavy toll of traditional British deference.[9] So did the postwar era's great British policy disasters: Suez, the 1967 sterling devaluation, the Callaghan Government's resort to the IMF in 1976, the poll tax, the BSE crisis, the sad and unloved Millennium Dome. It is hard to take blunderers, even honest and well-meaning blunderers, entirely at their own valuation. Deference is thus eroded. So is trust. The erosion of both deference and trust has, of course, been hastened by *That Was the Week That Was, Beyond the Fringe* and *Spitting Image*, by John Humphrys, Jeremy Paxman and David Dimbleby and by (in their different ways) the likes of Neil Hamilton and Jonathan Aitken. Most recently, multiple television channels, the Internet and e-mail have given millions of people access to information which enables them to challenge received wisdom and the voices of authority in politics as well as in medicine and the law.

The upshot is that politics—and especially government—becomes more difficult. Leakers leak. Secrets are harder to keep. Protests and demonstrations are easier to organise. Obedience ceases to be automatic. The facts underlying government decisions are far more likely to be challenged than in the past. Around-the-clock press, radio and television interviews mean that ministers and officials are more likely to contradict each other. In a culture that is already a culture of contestation, the sheer volume of contestation (in both senses of the word "volume") grows inexorably. Not least, the speed of modern scientific and technological development means that governments are more and more required to take vital decisions on the basis of imperfect knowledge and amidst a welter of conflicting expert advice. In the country of the blind, the one-eyed man is king. In the country where everyone is partially sighted, no one is king.

Any assessment of contemporary constitutional change in the UK needs to take into account this long-term change, mirrored in many other countries, in the tone, the texture, the "atmospherics", of modern political life.

IV

In the next chapter, we shall consider what all these changes, coming on top of one another, imply for the future of Britain's constitution; but, before we do that, we need to take note of the fact that, of course, amidst all this change much has remained the same. The UK constitution has changed, but not out of all recognition.

Most notably, the British system, at least at the national level, remains a predominantly government-centred system. The central government, based in Westminster and Whitehall, is still regarded—and still regards itself—as the Great Initiator, the Universal Problem Solver. Change swirls around government ministers, some of it initiated by themselves, but their sense of who they are and what they exist to do has so far changed remarkably little. Ministers seemed surprised, even affronted, when the Scottish Parliament in 1999 adopted its own policy for funding Scottish higher education and when the Welsh Assembly in 2000 forced the resignation of Alun Michael, the London government's preferred choice as Welsh First Secretary. They seemed equally surprised and even affronted when a majority of London's voters had the cheek, also in 2000, to choose Ken Livingstone as their first elected Mayor. Ministers, but not only ministers, seem to find it hard to take on board that power devolved is indeed just that: power devolved, power that is no longer in one's own hands, power that is more than likely to spin out of control. Ministers will eventually learn the new rules of the devolution game, but it is apparently going to take time.

Another feature of the traditional British constitution that remains unperturbed is the relatively insignificant role assigned to the House of Commons and that the House of Commons assigns to itself. Backbench MPs on the government side continue in the traditional manner to rebel from time to time, and ministers continue in the traditional manner to take note of who the rebels are, of how many of them there are and of whether or not their particular grievances are likely to resonate with the wider public. But there was scarcely any mention in Labour's 1997 manifesto of House of Commons reform, as distinct from House of Lords reform, and under the new government there has been no major overhaul, or even a minor overhaul, of the role that MPs play in the governmental process. Most government bills are still not subject to pre-legislative scrutiny, Standing Committees remain non-specialist, Select Committees remain mostly impotent. And so forth. The House of Commons remains essentially its old self.

So does the Monarchy. So does the role of interest groups; their relationship with the Blair Government, as with the Thatcher and Major governments, continues to be more of the arm's-length variety than the close-embrace variety. So, too, does the role of the civil service. If anything, the British civil service has gradually become more, rather than less, subservient to ministers over the past twenty years. Civil servants, save possibly those in the Foreign Office, appear to be even less ready than in the past to emerge as vigorous advocates of specific lines of policy. Civil servants define themselves more than in the past as administrators and managers rather than as policy advisers. In any case, some part of their policy-advising role has been usurped by Special Advisers appointed, usually from outside the civil service, by ministers.

Not the least important element of non-change in the system concerns the prevailing political culture, which remains overwhelmingly one of contestation rather than collaboration, of dissensus-seeking rather than consensus-seeking. Anyone listening to the *Today* programme on Radio 4 or viewing Prime Minister's Questions in the Commons on Wednesdays scarcely needs reminding of that. The present Prime Minister evidently finds the culture of contestation distasteful, but the apparent depth of his distaste is a good measure of the culture's continuing dominance. Inter-party co-operation has proved possible in Scotland and Wales, and up to a point in Northern Ireland, but it has been largely confined to co-operation between the parties making up coalition administrations. It shows few signs as yet of penetrating those countries' political cultures as a whole. At Westminster, the traditional Conservative-Labour clash still overwhelms such signs as there are of Labour-Liberal Democrat co-operation. In most of the United Kingdom most of the time, it is still a case of "politics as usual".

This chapter having focused separately on change and non-change, we now turn to the crucial task of trying to make sense of the combination of changes and non-changes that we have been describing. It is, to say the least of it, an intriguing combination. Does it amount, taken as a whole, to "a new constitutional settlement"? Does the United Kingdom, indeed, still *have* a constitution? Those are the central questions for our final chapter.

4. A NEW CONSTITUTIONAL SETTLEMENT?

So far in this book the word "constitution" has been used wholly descriptively. Countries have constitutions (and sometimes Constitutions); but constitutions, as defined in Chapter 1, are neither good nor bad, neither laudable nor deplorable: they merely exist, as sets of important rules. But, of course, the word "constitution" has other, more normative connotations. To say of a proposal that it is unconstitutional is normally not to say something neutral and purely descriptive about it. Normally it is to say that the change is unwelcome and undesirable, that it constitutes a breach of the existing constitutional rules, which are taken to have some prior claim on our loyalty and affections. Constitutional government is thought to be good government. Behaving unconstitutionally is thought to be behaving badly. Whether we like it or not, the word "constitution" carries a heavy load of evaluative and emotional baggage.

A glance at the relevant entries in the second edition of the *Oxford English Dictionary* helps make the point. For example, the dictionary quotes Lord Chesterfield as saying in one of his letters that "England is now the only monarchy in the world that can properly be said to have a constitution."[1] It is clear what Lord Chesterfield meant. He did not mean that no other monarchies had important rules, written or unwritten, for ordering their affairs. Rather, he meant that England (or Britain) was the only monarchy in the world whose important rules, whether written or unwritten, ensured that the monarch's power was limited: that the king was so constrained by his ministers, by Parliament and by the courts that he could not, even if he wished to, become a tyrant or oriental despot. It was, of course, in Lord Chesterfield's century, the 18th, that the notion of the tripartite "separation of powers" developed. The whole point of separating the executive, legislative and judicial powers was that each of the three branches of government was to be constrained by the other two. That was what Montesquieu and America's Founding Fathers, as well as Lord Chesterfield, had in mind when they spoke of constitutions and constitutional government. And constitutional government, in their view, was not a neutral state of affairs. It was a highly desirable state of affairs.

In the same century, another Englishman, Lord Bolingbroke, went further and offered a precise definition of "constitution". His definition also carries a much greater weight of meaning than the one used in these pages so far. Lord Bolingbroke wrote:

> By Constitution We mean, whenever We speak with Propriety and Exactness, that Assemblage of Laws, Institutions and Customs, derived from certain fix'd Principles of Reason . . . that compose the general System, according to which the Community hath agreed to be govern'd.[2]

Note the phrase "certain fix'd Principles of Reason". Lord Bolingbroke clearly meant that a constitution, in the proper sense of the term, should not merely comprise a more or less random assemblage of laws, institutions and customs but that it should also possess a certain coherence, that it should be derived, as he said, from certain fixed principles. A proper constitution, in other words, should, in his view, hang together. It should make sense. It should be able to be elucidated rationally. We shall return to this idea at the very end of this chapter.

II

One of the first things to be said about the twelve changes listed in Chapter 3 is that most of them are permanent. They will not be reversed. Most of them, in practical political terms, are almost certainly irreversible. The UK will not withdraw from the European Union. The Rome, Maastricht and Amsterdam Treaties will not be radically renegotiated. The judges are not about to abandon their practice of judicial review, nor can they avoid, even if they wanted to, interpreting Acts of Parliament and acts of public authorities in the light of the Human Rights Act. The Bank of England seems certain to retain control for the foreseeable future over the setting of UK interest rates. The powers devolved in 1999 to the Scottish Parliament and the Welsh Assembly are not about to be un-devolved. London is not about to be deprived of some kind of city-wide strategic authority. It seems most unlikely that the new electoral systems adopted for elections to the Scottish Parliament, the Welsh Assembly, the Greater London Authority and the European Parliament will be jettisoned in favour of a reversion to old-fashioned first-past-the post. All these changes now form part of the new United Kingdom constitution. They will be central features of our governmental arrangements for many generations to come. The traditional British constitution outlined in Chapter 2 of this book is dead. *Requiescat in pace.*

That said, a number of question-marks do, of course, remain. The most obvious concerns Northern Ireland. The Good Friday Agreement of 1998 exists. As these words are written, the Agreement is being implemented; both the Northern Ireland Assembly and the power-sharing Executive Authority are going about their business. The longer they go about their business, the more likely it is that they will continue to do so. But everyone knows that not everyone in Northern Ireland fully accepts the Agreement, that suspicions on both sides still run deep (and are not without substance) and that passionate debates persist, not only in Northern Ireland but on this side of the North Channel, about both the terms of the Agreement and the ways in which it is being implemented. The Agreement and the new power-sharing institutions associated with it could collapse at any time.

There must also be uncertainty about the future of local government, not so much about its internal workings (though there certainly is that), but about its place in the overall constitutional scheme of things. Both major parties claim they wish to restore the prestige, power and authority of local government; but neither party shows any practical signs of doing any such thing. Local government is weak, is becoming, if anything, weaker and shows no signs of being strengthened. Still, a revival of local government, though improbable, is possible, and anyone looking at the constitution in 2001 should not completely rule out that possibility. As regards referendums, we may, or may not, have a referendum on the euro; we may, or may not, have a referendum on changing the electoral system. Gradually over time we may, or may not, develop a general doctrine concerning when referendums should, and should not, be held. We are certainly a long way from having any such doctrine at the moment, but then thirty years ago we were a long way from having referendums at all. A question-mark also hangs over the future of the British party system, but that is a topic we will touch on below.

Thus, we have a number of permanent changes, already in place, and a number of changes that have taken place but whose consequences—as in the cases of Northern Ireland, local government, referendums and the party system—have yet to work themselves out. But, in addition, there are a number of future changes, either possible or probable, that any current assessment of the constitution has to take into account.

One is that, following a recommendation by the government and the success of a popular referendum, we may join the arrangements known as Economic and Monetary Union: the euro zone or "euroland". No one knows whether, or when, that will happen; but, if it does, it will be of momentous constitutional significance. If handing over control of UK interest rates to the Bank of England can reasonably be described as a constitutional change, how much greater will be the constitutional significance of handing over control of UK interest rates to the European Central Bank in Frankfurt. There are some who maintain that joining Economic and Monetary Union would undoubtedly be economically and politically important but would not entail major *constitutional* consequences. That argument is quite impossible to sustain, at least on the definition of "constitution" used in this book. Joining EMU would, beyond question, be to change one of the most important rules regulating the way the UK system operates and the relations between governors and governed in the UK. Protestations to the contrary border on the perverse.

Another possible change for the future concerns the system to be used for electing members to the United Kingdom Parliament. The Labour Party's manifesto at the time of the 1997 general election stated unequivocally: "We are committed to a referendum on the voting system for the House of Commons". However, the party's manifesto did not specify a date by which such a referendum would be held, and, as of early 2001, none had been. At the time of writing, it is still unclear whether a similar pledge will be included in the next Labour manifesto and, if so, when, if ever, it will be fulfilled.

How important a change in Britain's constitution any change in the electoral system would prove to be would depend on the precise nature of the new system adopted. It has been suggested, for example, that the current first-past-the-post system for UK parliamentary elections might be replaced by the alternative vote, under which electors are invited to indicate their preference-ordering among the individual candidates standing for the parties in each parliamentary constituency. Instead of the voter in, say, the Chelmsford West constituency putting a cross against the name of one and only one candidate in Chelmsford West, he or she would be invited to express preferences for all the candidates in order: 1, 2, 3, 4 and so on. If none of the candidates won an absolute majority after the first preferences had been counted, the second preferences of the candidate who had finished last would be added to the other candidates' first-preference totals, and so on until one or other of the candidates had 50 per cent or more of the total vote. The winning candidate could then claim, quite reasonably, that he or she was the preferred candidate—if not necessarily the first-choice candidate—of a majority of the local electorate.

The consequences of introducing the alternative vote in the UK are not altogether predictable. Simulations of the results of the 1983, 1987 and 1992 general elections suggest that the Conservative Party would still have won comfortably in every case, though the Liberal Democrats and their predecessors (the Liberals and Social Democrats in 1983 and 1987) would have won more seats. In 1997, when a large majority of the electorate clearly wished to oust the Conservatives in favour of Labour, the alternative vote would almost certainly have increased not only the Liberal Democrats' representation in Parliament but also the Labour Party's, because the supporters of both those parties would almost certainly have cast a majority of their second-preference votes in favour of the other anti-Conservative party.[3] The most one can say is that, in the event of very close elections between the two major parties, the probability is somewhat increased that, because of the expected increase in the size of the Liberal Democrats' parliamentary representation, no one party would have an overall majority in the House of Commons. In other words, the alternative vote would probably increase, though only marginally, the chances of "hung" Parliaments.

Compared with the alternative vote, the consequences of introducing a genuinely proportional system for Westminster elections, such as the additional-member system or the regional-list system, can be predicted with near certainty. Given the fact that PR systems are indeed proportional, and especially given the fact that, as described in the last chapter, the British party system has become increasingly fragmented in recent years, the effect of holding PR elections in the UK would almost certainly be to ensure, first, that no one political party ever again succeeded in winning an overall majority in the House of Commons and, second, that all future UK governments would, therefore, be minority governments or, more probably, coalition governments. The structure of political power in the UK would thus be transformed, and equally fundamental changes in the UK's political culture could be expected to follow. Whatever else it would be, the introduction of proportional representation in this country would not be a change somewhere on the fringes of our political system: it would be a change at its very core.

Another change that may, or may not, be in the offing concerns the creation of new governmental institutions for some or all of the English regions. Labour at the time of the 1997 general election was, or sounded, favourably disposed towards the idea. The party's manifesto acknowledged that demand for directly elected regional government varied widely from region to region and denied that Labour would add a new tier of government to the existing English system; but it added: "In time we will introduce legislation to allow the people, region by region, to decide in a referendum whether they want directly elected regional government." A White Paper published shortly after the new government came to power reaffirmed this commitment. So far, however, nothing of significance has happened, and opinion inside the Blair Government appears to be divided on how, and whether, to proceed. Nevertheless, several English regions, notably the North West, the North East and the South West are likely to continue to press for a measure of directly elected regional government; and the present UK government, or some other government at some time in the future, may decide to act. Were that to happen, yet another new political force within the British system would have been created.

Regional government in England is clearly some way off. Further reform of the House of Lords appears to be a good deal closer. If, as we noted in the last chapter, the Blair Government accepts the recommendations of the Wakeham Commission, or some reasonably close approximation to them, then the new Upper House, while it will not begin to rival the House of Commons, will certainly carry greater political weight than either the unreformed House of Lords or the interim, largely hereditary-free House of Lords that now exists. In the presence of a newly reformed body, ministers would, to an even greater extent than at present, have to factor the probable response of the Upper House into almost all of their political calculations, notably those concerning primary legislation.

Finally, it seems probable, though by no means certain, that the government's new Freedom of Information Act will not only have immediate, if limited, practical consequences but that it will, possibly more importantly, in time have the effect of increasing the public's and the media's expectations of how much information, and what kinds of information, should be available in the public domain. The Act's provisions are considerably more restrictive than most of those who campaigned for freedom of information would have liked, and many specific requests for the disclosure of government documents will almost certainly be turned down (certainly far more than under the American legislation of the same name). Even so, the onus in future will be on governments to show why information should not be made available rather than, as now, on the public to show why it should. The task of governing will thereby become just a little more complicated; the ability of voters and the media to intrude themselves into the decision-making process will, beyond doubt, be enhanced.

III

These changes are for the future. Also for the future are the relations between Scotland and England; but those relations are so important, and are potentially so troublesome, that they need to be considered at greater length. It seems all but inevitable that, sooner rather than later, serious tensions will develop in the relations between Edinburgh and London.

One source of tension, probably the least of them, will be the number of Scottish MPs who should be elected to the Westminster Parliament. At the moment, Scottish representation in the UK Parliament is inflated considerably beyond what the size of the Scottish population would suggest was appropriate. There are at present at Westminster, bluntly, too many Scotsmen. The average English MP represents roughly 70,000 electors, the average Scottish MP only roughly 55,000. This substantial numerical discrepancy was quite easily tolerated by English politicians so long as the Scots had little control over their own national affairs; but it became an obvious anomaly, and one impossible to justify, once it was clear that the Scots were to have their own Parliament. The Act establishing the Parliament accordingly provides that, from the time of the next redistribution of parliamentary boundaries, Scotland's representation at Westminster will be on the same numerical basis as England's. The Scots will no longer be overrepresented.

Even this reduction, however, is unlikely to remain acceptable indefinitely, given that Scotland's Westminster MPs now have such a drastically reduced role. They no longer participate in the making of most law relating to Scotland, and many of the matters that lead individual citizens to make contact with their local member of Parliament—health and housing, for example—no longer fall within the remit of Scotland's Westminster members. When substantial powers were devolved to the Stormont

Parliament in Northern Ireland in 1922, the number of the Province's Westminster MPs was reduced from 30 to 13 to reflect the new constitutional reality; and it is only a matter of time before pressure develops, probably from within the English Conservative Party, for a comparable reduction to be made in the case of Scotland.[4] A future Conservative government in London might well decide to legislate for precisely such a reduction. The Scots—and the British Labour Party—would not be pleased.

Far more serious as a potential source of Anglo-Scottish tension—it has already started to arise—is the part that Scotland's Westminster MPs are to play in the passage of proposed UK legislation relating only to England. It is not at all obvious that Scottish MPs should continue to be permitted to vote on legislation that affects only England when English MPs are barred by the new devolution arrangements from voting on legislation that affects only Scotland. The asymmetry seems on the face of it unjustifiable, and it is certainly highly visible. The important issue involved has become known as "the West Lothian question" after Tam Dalyell, the MP for West Lothian, who first drew attention to it in the 1970s; but in fact Gladstone in the late 19th century was fully aware of the issue and made provision for it in some versions of his proposed Irish home rule legislation.

The obvious solution, though some of the details might be difficult to implement in practice, would be simply to legislate to prohibit Scottish Westminster MPs from voting on items of English and English-and-Welsh legislation. The only objection to this solution, but it is a serious one, is that a UK government could find itself with a parliamentary majority large enough to pass UK legislation but not large enough to pass English and English-and-Welsh legislation. But UK governments are supposed to enjoy the confidence of the House of Commons, and the confidence of the House of Commons has always been taken to mean, or at least to include, the ability of the government of the day to enact its legislative programme. If, however, Scottish MPs could not vote on English and English-and-Welsh legislation, an elected UK government could conceivably find itself able to govern the UK but not, in effect, able to govern England and Wales. One of the principal buttresses of the traditional UK constitution would have collapsed.

It goes without saying that this issue, like the one about the number of Scottish MPs at Westminster, has a partisan dimension. Since the end of the Second World War, Conservative governments in the UK have invariably enjoyed the support of a majority of English and Welsh MPs (however well or badly the Conservatives have fared in Scotland). Moreover, every postwar Labour government has also enjoyed a purely English and Welsh majority. It is simply not true, though it seems widely to be believed, that Labour governments are always dependent, or have ever been dependent, wholly on the support of Scottish Labour MPs. However, given Labour's current predominance in Scotland and the Conservatives' virtual collapse there, it is certainly possible that at some time in the future a UK Labour government could come to power with an overall House of Commons majority but without enough English and Welsh MPs to enable it to pass purely English and Welsh legislation. It is therefore in the Conservative Party's interests to press for a ban on Scottish Westminster MPs voting on English and English-and-Welsh legislation (it has already begun to do so) and in the Labour Party's interests to resist any such a ban. The issue will not go away.[5]

Money is also bound, sooner or later, to be a source of serious friction between Edinburgh and London. In this connection, there are two separate issues. One is the current system under which the Scottish Parliament and Executive's revenues take the form overwhelmingly of a single (huge) block grant from London. The Scots, as we saw in the last chapter, determine how the money will be spent, but, apart from their modest tax-varying powers, they have no say whatsoever in how the money is raised. In this respect, the current devolution arrangements are conspicuously lopsided, and it seems inevitable that at some point the Scottish Parliament, perhaps controlled by a coalition of parties opposed to the governing party in London, will seek to repatriate some or all of Scotland's tax-raising powers. The cause of national autonomy, of full home rule, would seem to demand it. Disentangling the Scottish and English tax systems in a mutually satisfactory way would, needless to say, be a formidable task.

The other issue relating to money is less complicated but potentially even more divisive. For generations past, the Scots have enjoyed levels of per capita public spending considerably higher than those prevailing south of the border. In the financial year 1997–98, public spending in Scotland totalled £4,772 per head of population; in England it came to only £3,897 per head of population.[6] This bias in favour of the Scots was formerly justified on the ground that the Scots were, on average, poorer than the English and that equity demanded that more money should therefore be spent on them. But that argument no longer holds. Living standards in Scotland are now as high (or, in some parts of the country, as low) as those in England, and in the annual haggling that takes place between Edinburgh and London over the size of Scotland's block grant the Scots are going to find it harder and harder to defend their nation's privileged status. For the time being, with a Labour government in power in London and a Labour-Liberal Democrat administration in power in Edinburgh, the bargaining between the two sides, while it will always be tough, is likely to remain reasonably amicable. But the election of a Conservative government in London, with a Labour-led administration still in power in Scotland, could cause—almost certainly *would* cause—a sharp deterioration in relations between the two countries.

Nor would the so-called Barnett formula prove to be of any help. The Barnett formula is widely supposed on both sides of the border to be a convenient device for ensuring that Scotland and the Scots continue to receive, into the indefinite future, a disproportionate share of UK public expenditure. But it is no such thing—and never has been. On the contrary, the Barnett formula is a device for ensuring that, as the gap in living standards between Scotland and England closes, so also will close, in a gradual and orderly way, the gap between per capita public spending in Scotland and England. Moreover, the Barnett formula is not set in stone. It can be, and frequently has been, revised in order to take account of current circumstances, including the desire of London governments (of both parties) to win Scottish votes. The prospect is now in store, however, that one day a Conservative government will come to power in London, that that government will not be greatly interested in Scottish Conservative votes (there being so few of them) and that it will thereupon use its majority in the UK parliament to cut substantially Scotland's grant. It could well have majority support in England for doing so. The consequences of such a confrontation are easily imagined—or, if one prefers, are unimaginable.

The case of the block grant is, however, only a specific case of a more general problem. For the moment, the relations between the London government, which gave Scotland its devolved Parliament, and the Edinburgh government, which is enjoying the fruits of having the Parliament, are quite cordial. But that cannot last. Some day a Conservative government will come to power in London while some kind of administration involving the Labour Party and its allies remains in office in Edinburgh. Less probably, but perfectly possibly, a Labour government will remain in power in London but the Edinburgh Parliament will fall into the hands of some kind of anti- or non-Labour alliance, possibly involving the SNP. Sooner or later, "divided government" along these lines is certain to affect, almost certainly adversely, Anglo-Scottish political relations.

Moreover, the chances of a serious falling out between London and Edinburgh are substantially increased by the changes in the British party system that have already been referred to several times in these pages. We noted in the last chapter that, following the 1997 general election, the Conservative Party's Scottish representation at Westminster had been reduced to zero. The Conservatives' share of the vote in Scotland in 1997 was a mere 17.5 per cent (compared with nearly double that, 33.7 per cent, in England).[7] But what is even more important is a fact of United Kingdom politics that has attracted almost no attention from either British politicians or British political commentators, especially south of the border. It is possible that the politicians and the commentators are so reluctant to recognise the fact because its implications are so uncomfortable. The fact is that, not only have the Conservatives in recent years become a negligible force in United Kingdom elections north of the border, but they will almost certainly remain a negligible force for the indefinite future. In the 1950s, to go back half a century, the Conservatives won almost as many seats as the Labour Party in Scotland; they shared with Labour almost equally the representation of Glasgow. Those days are gone, almost certainly forever. For example, as we noted in the last chapter, at the 1970 general election the Conservatives won 23 Scottish seats in the UK Parliament, a wholly respectable number. A detailed analysis of those 23 Westminster seats—and their successor seats, since there have been extensive boundary changes since 1970—suggests that at a general election today or at any time in the near future the Conservatives could reasonably hope to regain, at most, about half a dozen of them. In other words, the Conservatives seem fated to remain for years to come, possibly for decades to come, a minority party, possibly a small minority party, in Scotland, in terms both of their share of Scotland's Westminster vote and of the number of Scotland's Westminster seats that they hold.

A conclusion of great significance ineluctably follows. The Conservative Party is bound some day to be returned to power at Westminster (possibly sooner rather than later). When that day comes, two things are almost certain to be true. First, the new Conservative government is almost certain to have little or no basis of electoral support in Scotland; and, second, the new Conservative administration in London is almost certain to find itself confronting a Scottish administration in Edinburgh that contains no Conservative representatives and that has little or no use for either the Conservative Party or its policies. Under those circumstances, some kind of major Anglo-Scottish collision seems all but inescapable. The Scottish Executive will have conscientious grounds for taking issue with the London-based executive. The Scottish Executive will, in addition, undoubtedly find it politically expedient to lay all of Scotland's problems at London's door. Just as American politicians have long run against Washington, so Scotland's politicians would then have every incentive to run against London.

It goes without saying that, with a Conservative government installed in London and an anti-Conservative administration installed in Edinburgh, the tensions between two centres, over money but not only over money, could become so severe as to call in question the future of the Union. The end of the 1990s and the early 2000s may, in retrospect, come to be seen as having constituted the honeymoon period in London-Edinburgh relations. The honeymoon could well end in marital bickering. It could end in divorce.

IV

It should be clear by now that many of the changes in our traditional constitution are permanent and irreversible. But it should also be clear that significant future changes may still occur and that, even with regard to many of the changes that have already taken place, their full consequences have yet to work themselves out. Scotland is one instance. Britain's relations with Europe are another. Freedom of information is a third. Others can easily be identified. For example, it is not yet clear whether the newly enhanced role of the British judiciary—in regard to both judicial review and the Human Rights Act—will or will not lead to our judiciary's becoming to some degree "politicised", whether as a result of the political vetting of judicial appointments or as a result of the judges increasingly becoming caught up in public, and inevitably partisan, controversy.

In other words, the United Kingdom's constitution is, and remains, in flux. No one can predict with confidence what its appearance will be in a few years' time, let alone a few decades' time. Our politicians will have to learn, are already having to learn, new ways of working. Our citizens will have to learn, are already having to learn, new ways of responding to the ways in which our politicians work. We face, to say the least of it, an uncertain constitutional future. With the exceptions of the disempowerment of the House of Lords in 1911 and the secession of most of Ireland in the early 1920s, the UK constitution changed remarkably little between about 1870 and 1970. That period of prolonged stability is now over. It is not about to be followed by another one.

That point, although obvious, is worth emphasising because it is sometimes suggested that, now that the changes introduced by the post-1997 Labour government have been successfully put in place, we have not only acquired a new constitution but one that will have the same validity and the same durability as the old one. The terms of reference of the Royal Commission on the Reform of the House of Lords, for instance, referred to the UK's new "constitutional settlement", and some ministers have been heard to use the same phrase. But that is to be altogether too optimistic. The UK constitution remains unsettled, profoundly unsettled. We have, if anything, a new constitutional unsettlement.

V

If that were all that could be said, we would have no option at this point but to throw up our hands, settle back and await developments. But there is, fortunately, a good deal more to be said. Some features of Britain's new political arrangements are beginning, quite clearly, to emerge from the fog of uncertainty.

One concerns that ancient issue in British politics: the one concerning the relationship between governors and governed, the one between, so to speak, Caius Martius and the common people of Rome. That relationship, under the traditional British constitution, was to be strictly a division-of-labour, us-and-them relationship. The political class was to govern. The people were to be the passive recipients of government, irrespective of whether the quality of that government was good or bad (as the case might be). To be sure, if the government were bad enough, it could be removed in due course by the common people, giving voice to "their vulgar wisdoms". But otherwise the mass of the people were to be kept strictly out of it.

However, subtly, imperceptibly and without much attention having been paid to the fact, that relationship—or at least people's expectations of that relationship—has begun to change. There are now referendums from time to time. The referendum as a political device has become legitimate. There are calls for even more referendums to be held in the future. Referendums are to be held not merely on the electoral system, the euro and the possibility of introducing new forms of elected government into the English regions but also on how the internal affairs of local authorities are to be organised. There are not only to be referendums: public consultation has become all the rage, with local authorities, health authorities and other bodies enjoined by governments of both political persuasions to consult the public as part of their processes of decision making. The people, to an extent that would horrify the ghost of Caius Martius, are in fashion. The focus group is not only the voice of God: it is regarded as being God's authentic voice, a voice, therefore, to be listened to with a reverence approaching awe.

A changed attitude towards the relationship between governors and governed in any country is a change in the constitution of that country, whether or not the change is publicly acknowledged and whether or not the change is codified in either law or a written Constitution. That such a change has taken place in the UK is beyond question. The Major Government's Citizen's Charters, with their codifications of citizens' rights *vis-à-vis* public authorities, testify to the change that has taken place. So do a wide variety of the public pronouncements of Tony Blair and his cabinet colleagues. This was to be, and still is to be, a listening government, a government in intimate touch with the people, not merely on vote-maximising grounds but on normative grounds. Labour's 1997 manifesto promised that a Labour government would work as "partners . . . with our people". Ministers and their officials have since spoken frequently of the need "to revitalise democracy", by which is meant the need to re-engage ordinary people in the life of their communities and of the nation as a whole.

All of this is, without doubt, sincerely meant. Tony Blair, in particular, gives the impression, as John Major did before him, of wishing to reconnect (if they ever were connected) the mass of ordinary people with their government and their governing institutions. There is only one problem. It has not worked. The politicians may have changed their beliefs about the proper role of the people. The people, however, have not changed their beliefs about politicians and about what politicians ought to be doing on their behalf. Attempts to reconnect the general public with the political class have led, if anything, to further disconnection.

Opinion polls bearing on these issues offer us one kind of indicator, but another and possibly better indicator is provided by turnout in elections. It is a simple fact that, as the rhetoric of reconnection and revitalisation has been heightened, the willingness of ordinary people to participate in the electoral process has continuously declined. Needless to say, the continuous decline has been accompanied by even more strenuous efforts at reconnection and revitalisation. The British political elite is obviously aware that something has gone wrong with the governors/governed relationship and that there has developed in the UK what might be called "a paradox of participation". The more people are invited to participate, the less inclined they are to do so.

The figures are well known. The decline in the numbers voting at UK general elections has been gradual and fairly gentle and would not by itself be a cause for concern (though turnout at the 1997 general election, 71.5 per cent, was the lowest since 1935). But turnout at most other forms of election in recent years has ranged from the disappointing to the abysmal. A respectable number of Scots, 60.2 per cent, voted in the 1997 Scottish devolution referendum, but the turnout in the Welsh referendum on devolution was only 50.1 per cent and a mere 34.0 per cent of Londoners bothered to vote in the 1998 referendum that created the new Greater London Authority. In Scotland turnout in the first elections to the new Parliament in 1999 was again respectable, 58.9 per cent, but in Wales only 46.3 per cent of the eligible electorate bothered to vote, and in the elections to the European Parliament, held on the same day, the turnout was a derisory 24.1 per cent, the lowest in the EU.[8] The proportion of people voting in local elections, which used to hover somewhere above 40 per cent, now seldom exceeds 30 per cent. Voting in referendums and elections in the UK, apart from general elections, shows every sign of becoming a minority activity.

All kinds of reasons could be given to explain these low levels of electoral participation, and some of them undoubtedly have a degree of validity. People feel less passionately about politics than they did in the immediate postwar period (and may do again at moments of national crisis). Voting is less "tribal" than it once was. Except on Europe, the Conservative and Labour parties are closer together in the 2000s than they were at any time in the 1970s and 1980s. (At any rate most voters believe that they are.) Perhaps most important, most people clearly believe there is not much at stake at most referendums and elections apart from general elections. It does not matter greatly, in their eyes, who represents them on the local council (which, in any case, has lost much of its autonomy); it matters even less who represents them in the European Parliament (which, voters seem vaguely to recognise, is not a very influential body). Most UK referendums and elections are clearly what political scientists call "second order" elections. It is significant that turnout was higher both at the Scottish devolution referendum and at the first elections to the Scottish Parliament. In Scotland, people apparently believed there *was* something at stake.

All those explanations are telling. It is hard to deny the truth of any of them. But perhaps the current paradox of participation has a more profound meaning. Members of the political class have come in recent years to believe that they have a moral duty to give the British people the final word on a wide variety of occasions, and they have also come to believe that the British people have a passionate desire to be given the final word. But perhaps the whole of the political class is wrong. Perhaps the people *do* want to be listened to and *do* want those in government to recognise and meet their needs; but perhaps, otherwise, they simply want to be left alone to get on with their lives. Politicians love politics. There is not much evidence that most ordinary people do. Perhaps the politicians, in their anxiety to please, are projecting their own enthusiasm for political activity onto a mass of ordinary people who are far from sharing their enthusiasm. That would certainly help to explain why the more referendums and elections there are, the smaller the numbers of people who bother to vote in them.

The same point can be put even more sharply. Under the traditional British constitution, the governors governed and the people allowed themselves to be governed, except once in every four or five years when they went to the polls to pass their verdict on how well or badly the current governors had performed. What seems to have happened is that the governors in Britain are no longer as convinced as they were that they have a moral right to govern, while, for their part, the people remain stolidly of the view that, once they have chosen the government at a general election, the governors, having been chosen, should simply get on with it. The people do, it seems, want to vote once in every four or five years and but then want to be left alone until the next election comes round. They do want to be able to voice "their vulgar wisdoms" from time to time, but they do not want to be full-time, non-stop, hyperactive citizens. If this analysis is correct, or even partially correct, Caius Martius would be at once relieved to see the common people so modest and, at the same time, contemptuous of the members of the Roman Senate for having given way so readily to what they wrongly believed to be the people's demands.

It is probably too late to reduce significantly the number of elections that are held in the UK, but politicians in all parties might wish to consider whether they should continue to multiply, as they seem to want to do, the sheer number of referendums and elections that take place. They might also wish to consider whether the number of actual polling days could not be substantially reduced. The best way of revitalising British democracy might be to have less of it. It would be sad if our politicians came to be seen as nothing more than a pestilential nuisance.

The people's role in the constitution has thus been subtly but substantially altered, if not in ways that the people themselves seem altogether to like. But there has also taken place an additional and far less subtle change in the basis of our constitution. We stressed repeatedly in Chapter 2 that the essence of our traditional constitution was the concentration of political power. Ours was, in an extreme form, a government-centred constitution. To a considerable extent, it still is. The system of government within the worlds of Whitehall and Westminster—with Whitehall deliberately put first—has changed relatively little in recent years; but large changes have been going on outside. Put simply, while historically the government of the day in the United Kingdom had few rivals to its power and authority, the government under our new arrangements has several such rivals. New centres of autonomous power have come into being. We mentioned each of them individually in the last chapter, but it is important to see the effect that they are having, collectively, on the way the UK is governed.

The European Union—its Council of Ministers, its Commission, its Court of Justice and to a lesser extent its Parliament—is now a political force that no one in British government can even contemplate disregarding. The traffic of ministers and officials, not to mention phone calls, faxes and e-mails, is now at least as heavy between some Whitehall departments and Brussels as it is within Whitehall itself. The European Union is no longer, if it ever was, some semi-detached adjunct to the British political system; it is an integral part of it. No description of the British constitution in the early 2000s could be complete without including the EU as one of its principal components. If any political leader's constituency is taken to include all the people with whom he or she must transact formal governmental business, then other EU leaders and EU officials now form part of the working constituency of every British cabinet minister. Ministers newly appointed to the government are often shocked to discover how constrained they are by the EU and what a large volume of EU-related business they have to transact.

The two other most conspicuous centres of power under our new constitution are, of course, to be found in Edinburgh and Cardiff. London's writ used to run throughout Great Britain (and after 1972 throughout the United Kingdom). Now, for a wide range of purposes, it stops at either Carter Bar or the Severn Bridge. Legislation that was once United Kingdom legislation is increasingly English or English-and-Welsh legislation. If the Scottish Parliament wishes to abolish fees in Scottish higher education, it is free to do precisely that. Moreover, the effects of Scottish legislation are felt not only in Scotland; Whitehall now has to take note of the probable effects of Scottish legislation on English interests, including, as it happens, the interests of university students. A simple measure of the importance that the new Scottish and Welsh institutions have already acquired is that, whereas in the UK there used to be only one political career ladder, propped up against the walls of the Palace of Westminster, there are now at least three, one in London but also two others in Edinburgh and Cardiff. New institutions, new power bases. Donald Dewar will be remembered as Scotland's first First Minister, not as a former Secretary of State for Scotland (a post that, in any case, is likely soon to be abolished).

The judiciary is also now a living presence in the constitution in a way that it was not before. The custom and practice of judicial review seems likely to expand (it will certainly not contract); and the Human Rights Act already imposes additional responsibilities on judges throughout the UK. So long as Parliament acted as, in effect, the agent of the executive, and so long as the judiciary was also inclined to defer to the executive, then Britain's constitution could not be said to be, and never was said to be, a separation-of-powers constitution. As regards the relations between the executive and the legislature, ours is still not that kind of constitution; but, as regards the relations between the executive and the judiciary, it has latterly become considerably more of one. Checks and balances are the hallmark of a separation-of-powers constitution. The judiciary is now willing and able to check the executive in a fashion unprecedented for at least a century. Another new power base.

This list of new power bases could be extended to include, most notably, the Bank of England, the newly cantankerous House of Lords and the Mayor of London. From the list, however, would have to be subtracted, at least for the time being, local government. But, however the list were tabulated, and however the various new power bases were weighed, it is abundantly clear that the British system is now a far less government-centred system than it was. Power in the state is far more widely diffused. Whatever Dicey may have said a century ago, there is no longer a single "sovereign" anywhere within our constitution.

One important consequence should be mentioned straightaway. The point was emphasised in Chapter 2 that a central feature of the traditional British constitution, almost its defining feature, was the way in which, by concentrating power and authority in the government of the day, it enabled the people, in their role as voters, to hold the government to account. Whatever else it was, British government was accountable government. Everyone knew who the government was; everyone knew that it was responsible, by and large, for everything that did, and did not, happen in the country. As the Chicago professor said, the line of authority between people and government in Britain rose singly and directly and descended singly and directly. The line of authority and responsibility was, as he put it, "undivided and crystal-clear".[9]

Not any longer. Diffused power, especially if it is widely diffused power, is apt in practice to be unaccountable power—or, at the least, power that is not in any straightforward way accountable to the people. The European Union, the judiciary, the Bank of England, parliaments and assemblies in Scotland, Wales and Northern Ireland, even the House of Lords to some extent—all are now licensed power-holders in the UK system. Who therefore can be held to account for the malaise in British agriculture? Who, if anyone, can be held to account for high interest rates in the UK, leading to a strong pound, leading to a decline in UK manufacturing industry? Once upon a time, it was "them", the government. But who is it now? The Chancellor of the Exchequer, for setting a low inflation target which the Bank of England is expected to hit? The Bank itself, which actually sets the rates? Someone, somewhere, in Europe? No one seems to know. Certainly few voters believe they know. An additional explanation for the voter apathy referred to above is almost certainly voter bewilderment and, more precisely, a belief on the part of voters that they have been to a large extent, in effect, disenfranchised. Power in the system has not only been dispersed: it has been dispersed away from them; it has spun out of *their* control. Small wonder that many of them are resentful.

VI

The new arrangements having been described and analysed, it is time to return to the two constitutional archetypes set out in

Chapter 1: the power-sharing archetype and the power-hoarding archetype. To which, if either, does the new British system more closely conform?

It clearly does not conform to the power-sharing archetype. It will be remembered that the key features of that archetype included not only a pluralist and fragmented structure of political institutions but also a political culture of power sharing and consensus seeking. It was an archetype typically characterised by multi-party systems, coalition governments and strong, or at least not negligible, parliaments. In any power-sharing system, the political class not only recognised the practical necessity of compromising with their allies and opponents in the interests of reaching inter-party agreements; they also believed that such agreements, based on such compromises, were intrinsically desirable. No one, if at all possible, was to be an outright winner; no one, if at all possible, was to be an outright loser. The principles of proportionality and inclusivity were to prevail.

The new British constitution, despite all the changes that have taken place, is clearly unrecognisable in those terms. To be sure, elements of the power-sharing archetype are evident in the new arrangements for Northern Ireland, and there are signs in both Scotland and Wales that power-sharing arrangements and a power-sharing culture may emerge in time; the practice of coalition government may eventually lead to coalition-mindedness. But, everywhere else in the system, all is as it was before. The Westminster government is single-party government. The central political principle is still the principle of winner take all. The political culture remains a culture of contestation. No one observing the Westminster Parliament in action or watching *Question Time* on television could imagine that Britain had, politically, entered a new era of civility and good feelings.

But neither does the UK system any longer conform to the power-hoarding archetype. It is alleged that some leading Labour politicians and advisers wish that it did. But it does not. The central government's successive failures to get its way in Scotland ought to have proved that. So should the debacle over the leadership of the Welsh Assembly (not to mention the even more spectacular debacle over the first London mayoral election). The single most important feature of the power-hoarding archetype was that political power was concentrated in the hands of a few individuals and institutions; there was, in some reasonable sense of the term, a "sovereign". But that is no longer the case. As we have seen, power in the British system is now far more highly fragmented and dispersed than it was in the past. To the age-old question "Who is in charge?" there is no longer in the UK, as there used to be, a straightforward and unequivocal answer. Under a wide range of headings, power over the past three decades has either been given away or taken away. In short, the British constitution has ceased to be a power-hoarding constitution without having become a power-sharing constitution.

What, then, is it? How is one to describe a system in which power is parcelled out but, far from being shared, is, or is likely to be, highly contested? A single term is probably required, if only to distinguish the new British arrangements from our two archetypes and also from the political systems of other countries.

The term that suggests itself, on the model of power-sharing and power-hoarding, is "power-fractionated". To fractionate is to break up, to break into fragments, to disrupt, to create a breach or a fissure. The term seems apt, partly because over recent decades there has occurred a decisive break with the past, but also because over the same decades political power and authority in Britain have, as we have seen, been to a considerable extent broken up into fractions or fragments. The fact that the fractions and fragments are of manifestly unequal size makes the physical metaphor, if anything, even more suggestive. The additional fact that the word "fraction" is etymologically linked to the word "faction" adds an appropriately disputatious note to the overall conception.

VII

One of the most striking features of the new United Kingdom constitution is that no one designed it. No one planned it. There was no United Kingdom constitutional convention, with delegates from Scotland, Wales, Northern Ireland and the English regions solemnly assembled in, say, Westminster Hall. No one of influence suggested that there should be the British equivalent of Philadelphia in 1787 or Bonn in 1948–49. This country has never had a defining constitutional moment. It still has not had one.

Some of the changes listed in Chapter 3—notably the fragmentation of the British party system—simply happened, without anyone in particular having willed them. Others—notably Britain's accession to the European Economic Community, the holding of *ad hoc* referendums and the handing over to the Bank of England of control over UK interest rates—were consciously willed, but without much thought being given to their constitutional implications. The greater number—notably devolution to Scotland, Wales and Northern Ireland, the reform of the House of Lords and the passage of the Human Rights Act—were willed by the Blair Government and were recognised as constituting, in effect, constitutional amendments. But it goes without saying that we still lack a codified capital-C Constitution and, more important, that no one has yet been in a position to write, in the style of America's Founding Fathers, a volume of *Federalist Papers* expounding the new constitution and extolling its virtues.

The reason there is no volume of *Federalist Papers* is straightforward. No one could write such a volume. And the reason no one could write such a volume is that the new constitution lacks not only a planner but a plan. The traditional United Kingdom constitution also did not have a planner, but it did have a plan, or at least a set of reasonably coherent organising principles: the concentration of power, the division of labour between governors and governed, electoral accountability and so forth. The detail might be obscure, but the basic ground plan, of almost cruciform-like simplicity, was plain for all to see. The traditional constitution closely resembled Lincoln or Durham cathedrals; the new constitution more closely resembles those of Cordoba or Seville—or possibly a builder's yard.

One simple clue to the lack of sustained thought that has gone into the process of British constitutional change is the extent to which power accumulating and power shedding have gone on more or less simultaneously. On the one hand, local government has been deprived of many of its functions and much of its autonomy, the House of Commons has been kept rigorously in its place, and the impending reform of the House of Lords, whatever else it does, will not set up a second chamber of German-like or United States-like importance. But, on the other hand, the Blair Government's own claims to have been willing to delegate power, to shed it, are almost entirely justified. The charge of control-freakery is impossible to sustain against an administration that has delegated power to the Bank of England, London, Scotland, Wales and Northern Ireland, that has strengthened the power of the judiciary by putting the Human Rights Act on the statute book and that has proved substantially more willing than any of its predecessors to share power with the European Union and the individual EU member states.

What, we must ask, would Lord Bolingbroke make of it all? The short answer is: not much. On his definition of the word "constitution", the constitution of a country should not merely comprise an "Assemblage of Laws, Institutions and Customs": that assemblage of laws, institutions and customs should itself be "derived from certain fix'd Principles of Reason". The United Kingdom today certainly possesses a constitution in the purely descriptive sense of having a set of rules regulating the relations among the different parts of the government and the relations between the different parts of the government and the people. However, it does not even begin to possess a constitution in Lord Bolingbroke's sense of the term. The new United Kingdom constitution cannot be said to be derived from certain fixed principles of reason—or indeed from any principles at all. Does that matter? Who knows? We shall see in due course.

NOTES

Chapter 1. Two Constitutional Archetypes

[1] Jonathan Steinberg, *Why Switzerland?*, 2nd edn. (Cambridge: Cambridge University Press, 1996), p. 37.

[2] The passages on the Netherlands that follow are based largely on Rudy B. Andeweg and Galen A. Irwin, *Dutch Government and Politics* (Basingstoke, Hants.: Macmillan, 1993); but see also Rudy B. Andeweg, "From Dutch Disease to Dutch Model?—Consensus Government in Practice", *Parliamentary Affairs*, 53 (October 2000), 697–709, Rudy B. Andeweg, "The Netherlands" in Jean Blondel and Ferdinand Müller-Rommel, *Cabinets in Western Europe*, 2nd edn. (Basingstoke, Hants.: Macmillan, 1997), Ken Gladdish, *Governing from the Centre: Politics and Policy-Making in the Netherlands* (London: Hurst, 1991), Robert A. Dahl and Edward R. Tufte, *Size and Democracy* (Stanford, Calif.: Stanford University Press, 1974) and Hans Daalder, "The Netherlands: Opposition in a Segmented Society" in Robert A. Dahl, ed., *Political Oppositions in Western Democracies* (New Haven, Conn.: Yale University Press, 1966).

[3] On consociational democracy in general, and Dutch politics and government in particular, see Arend Lijphart, *The Politics of Accommodation: Pluralism and Democracy in the Netherlands*, 2nd edn. (Berkeley, Calif.: University of California Press, 1975).

[4] Andeweg and Irwin, *Dutch Government and Politics*, p. 37.

[5] *ibid.*, p. 168.

[6] *ibid.*, p. 239.

Chapter 2. The British Tradition and Its Logic

[1] The passage can be found towards the beginning of the play, in Act 1, Scene 1.

[2] The figures quoted in the text relate to 1946–47 and 1968–69. They are drawn from Gerald Rhodes, "Local Government Finance 1918–1966" in *Local Government Finance: Appendix 6 to the Report of the Committee of Inquiry under the Chairmanship of Frank Layfield Esq QC: The Relationship between Central and Local Government: Evidence and Commissioned Work* (London: Her Majesty's Stationery Office, 1976), p. 154, Table 1.

[3] Quoted in Peter Hennessy, *Whitehall* (London: Secker & Warburg, 1989), p. 346.

[4] L.S. Amery, *Thoughts on the Constitution*, 2nd edn. (London: Oxford University Press, 1964), pp. 20–21.

[5] Quoted in Philip Goodhart, *Referendum* (London: Tom Stacey, 1971), p. 33.

[6] Quoted by Vernon Bogdanor, "Western Europe" in David Butler and Austin Ranney, eds., *Referendums Around the World: The Growing Use of Direct Democracy* (Washington, D.C.: AEI Press, 1994), p. 36.

[7] D.E. Butler, *The Electoral System in Britain since 1918*, 2nd edn. (Oxford: Clarendon Press, 1963), p. 5.

[8] The electorate in 1900 numbered 6,730,509. In 1929, the year of the first election when women had the franchise on the same basis as men, it numbered 28,850,870. See David Butler and Gareth Butler, *Twentieth-Century British Political Facts, 1900–2000*, 8th edn. (Basingstoke, Hants.: Macmillan, 2000), pp. 233–35.

[9] John Stuart Mill, "Considerations on Representative Government" in *On Liberty and Other Essays*, edited by John Gray (Oxford: Oxford University Press, 1991), p. 240.

[10] William Edward Hearn quoted by L.S. Amery, *Thoughts on the Constitution*, p. 2.

[11] The estimates in the text have been culled from a variety of secondary sources, all of which relate to specific phases of the Irish conflict rather than to the conflict as a whole. It has so far proved impossible to uncover an authoritative source of information on the total number of people killed during the relevant decade.

[12] Relief agencies' estimate quoted in Thomas Hennessy, *A History of Northern Ireland 1920–1996* (Basingstoke, Hants.: Macmillan, 1997), p. 11.

[13] See Sven Steinmo, *Taxation and Democracy: Swedish, British and American Approaches to Financing the Modern State* (New Haven, Conn.: Yale University Press, 1993). Steinmo writes that "the major distinguishing characteristic of the British tax system is its instability. The British tax system changes faster, more frequently, and more radically than any other tax system I have observed" (p. 44).

[14] Herman Finer, *The Major Governments of Modern Europe* (Evanston, Ill.: Row, Peterson, 1960), p. 67.

[15] Anthony King, "Distrust of Government: Explaining American Exceptionalism" in Susan J. Pharr and Robert D. Putnam, *Disaffected Democracies: What's Troubling the Trilateral Countries?* (Princeton, N.J.: Princeton University Press, 2000), p. 95.

Chapter 3. The United Kingdom Constitution Amended

[1] Harry Eckstein, "The British Political System" in Samuel H. Beer and Adam B. Ulam, eds., *Patterns of Government: Major Political Systems of Europe*, 2nd edn. (New York: Random House, 1962), pp. 73–74.

[2] André Mathiot, *The British Political System*, trans. Jennifer S. Hines (London: Hogarth Press, 1958), p. 335.

[3] On "adversarial politics" (a term not currently much in fashion), see, in particular, S.E. Finer, ed., *Adversary Politics and Electoral Reform* (London: Anthony Wigram, 1975).

[4] Office for National Statistics, *Housebuilding Completions: By Sector, 1945–1998: Social Trends Data Set* [on line dataset: ST301001, http://www.statistics.gov.uk].

[5] Figures cited in Bill Jones, Dennis Kavanagh, Michael Moran and Philip Norton, *Politics UK*, 4th edn. (Harlow, Essex: Longman, 2001), p. 511.

[6] Totals calculated from David Butler and Gareth Butler, *Twentieth-Century British Political Facts*, 8th edn. (Basingstoke, Hants.: Macmillan, 2000), pp. 237–39.

[7] Data on votes cast and seats won in parliamentary elections in England, Scotland and Wales since 1979 can be found in the series of Nuffield College election studies by David Butler and Dennis Kavanagh: *The British General Election of 1979* (London: Macmillan, 1980), p. 357, *The British General Election of 1983* (London: Macmillan, 1984), p. 301, *The British General Election of 1987* (Basingstoke, Hants: Macmillan, 1988), p. 284, *The British General Election of 1992* (Basingstoke, Hants.: Macmillan, 1992), p. 286 and *The British General Election of 1997* (Basingstoke, Hants.: Macmillan, 1997), p. 256.

[8] *The Belfast Agreement: An Agreement Reached at the Multi-Party Talks on Northern Ireland*, Cm. 3883 (London: Stationery Office, 1998), p. 5.
[9] On the "romantic revolution", see Samuel H. Beer, *Britain Against Itself: The Political Contradictions of Collectivism* (New York: W.W. Norton, 1982), Chap. 4.

Chapter 4. A New Constitutional Settlement?

[1] "Constitution", *Oxford English Dictionary*, 2nd edn., Vol. 3 (Oxford: Oxford University Press, 1989), p. 790.
[2] *ibid.*
[3] The simulations are noted briefly in the Jenkins Report: *The Report of the Independent Commission on the Voting System*, Cm. 4090–1 (London: Stationery Office, 1998), pp. 25–26.
[4] The Northern Ireland figures have been calculated from F.W.S. Craig, *British Parliamentary Election Results 1885–1918*, 2nd edn. (Aldershot, Hants.: Dartmouth, 1989) and F.W.S. Craig, *British Parliamentary Election Results 1918–1949*, 3rd edn. (Chichester, Sussex: Parliamentary Research Services, 1983).
[5] The issue is further complicated by the presence of Northern Ireland MPs at Westminster. If a majority of them chose to back the Conservatives in a finely balanced parliament, a Labour government could find it even more difficult to pass purely English and Welsh legislation. All Labour governments with small overall majorities would, of course, find themselves in a precarious position with regard to English and Welsh legislation.
[6] HM Treasury, *Public Expenditure Statistical Analyses 1999–2000*, Cm. 4201 (London: Stationery Office, 1999), Section 8, Table 8.1 and Tables 8.2B-8.6B
[7] David Butler and Dennis Kavanagh, *The British General Election of 1997* (Basingstoke, Hants.: Macmillan, 1997), p. 256.
[8] The turnout figures can be found in David Butler and Gareth Butler, *Twentieth-Century British Political Facts 1900–2000*, 8th edn. (Basingstoke, Hants.: Macmillan, 2000), pp. 239 [1997 general election], p. 458 [Scottish referendum], p. 460 [Welsh referendum], p. 485 [London referendum], p. 459 [Scottish Parliament elections], p. 460 [Welsh Assembly elections] and p. 514 [1999 European Parliament elections].
[9] See above p. 48.

INDEX

Index